Uncommon Threads

The Ohio Quilt Series

Ricky Clark, Ellice Ronsheim, and Donna Sue Groves, series editors

Quilts of the Ohio Western Reserve, by Ricky Clark

Uncommon Threads: Ohio's Art Quilt Revolution, by Gayle A. Pritchard

Uncommon Threads

Ohio's Art Quilt Revolution

GAYLE A. PRITCHARD, 1957

Ohio University Press

ATHENS

Ohio University Press, Athens, Ohio 45701
www.ohio.edu/oupress
© 2006 by Ohio University Press

Printed in China

Ohio University Press books are printed on acid-free paper ⊗ ™

14 13 12 11 10 09 08 07 06   5 4 3 2 1

Cover art: *Reach for the Stars, 2004.* Cynthia Lockhart. 51" x 67".
Cottons, blends, rayon, taffeta, lamé, leather, suede, metallic
cording, braid and fabrics. Machine-pieced, appliquéd, embellished, hand-stitched French bias. Photo by Jay Yocis.

Library of Congress Cataloging-in-Publication Data
Pritchard, Gayle A., 1957–
  Uncommon threads : Ohio's art quilt revolution / Gayle A.
Pritchard.
      p. cm. — (The Ohio quilt series)
  Includes bibliographical references and index.
  ISBN-13: 978-0-8214-1706-5 (pbk. : alk. paper)
  ISBN-10: 0-8214-1706-1 (pbk. : alk. paper)
  1. Art quilts—Ohio—History—20th century. 2. Art quilts—
Ohio—History—21st century. I. Title.
  NK9112.P75 2006
  746.4609771—dc22
                    2006018931

Publication of *Uncommon Threads: Ohio's Art Quilt Revolution* has been made possible in part by the generous financial support of the North East Ohio Regional Quilt Council.

The Vowel Book: Table of Contents, 1995. Clare Murray.
15" x 17". Silk screen, stamping, painting, machine
stitching on canvas. Photo by John Seyfried.

Contents

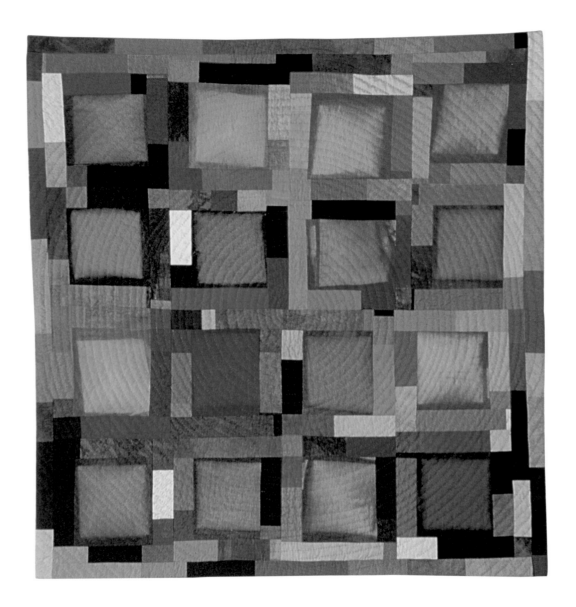

Color Blocks #35, 1993. Nancy Crow. 34.5" x 36.5". Cotton, hand-dyed by the artist, resist-dyed squares by Lunn Fabrics. Cut and machine-pieced by the artist. Hand-quilted by Marie Moore with pattern marked by the artist. As Crow's improvisational approach developed, she says, "I kept practicing until I taught myself to cut shapes directly out of the fabric without templates, without even knowing ahead of time what the overall composition might be." She has kept this work in her personal collection. A detail was used on the cover of *The Complete Collected Poems of Maya Angelou*. Photo by J. Kevin Fitzsimons.

Preface and Acknowledgments

The initial impetus for writing the untold story of the emergence and evolution of the art quilt movement in Ohio came as the result of a stimulating discussion during a symposium held in Oberlin, Ohio, in 2002. Entitled "Pathways and Perspectives," the symposium was a natural culmination of the Artist as Quiltmaker exhibition I had curated at the Firelands Association for the Visual Arts (FAVA) that same year. In celebration of twenty years of exhibiting art quilts, all previous Artist as Quiltmaker exhibition jurors, along with exhibition founder Ricky Clark, were invited to attend the symposium to discuss with an audience the history of the exhibit and the evolution and future of the art quilt.[1]

Inspired, I decided to dig deeper into the remarkable story of how their contributions eventually came to create the art quilt movement in Ohio. In expanding my research for *Uncommon Threads: Ohio's Art Quilt Revolution,* two questions kept floating through my mind: "Why Ohio?" and "What was going on in Ohio during the '70s that led to the emergence of the art quilt movement?" I was searching for the obvious: big events and larger-than-life people. What I found instead were the marks of individuals pursuing their work, finding their way, and, eventually, finding each other. It was through this confluence of independent individuals that the larger synergistic movement was born.

I am deeply grateful to all the participants in this story for their endless patience with my interview questions and follow-up e-mails and for the generous giving of their time, searching for and sharing personal materials. Most of all, I celebrate the focus and persistence all of them have brought to their own work. They have created a legacy for all of us. I am honored to tell their stories.

I would also like to acknowledge the following with special thanks for their support and assistance: Judi Warren Blaydon, Tafi Brown, Lois Carroll, Nancy Crow, Hilary Fletcher, Linda Fowler,

"Pathways and Perspectives" Symposium, June 8, 2002, Firelands Association for the Visual Arts, Oberlin. Artist as Quiltmaker founder Ricky Clark and former exhibition jurors gather to discuss the evolution of the art quilt over the past twenty years. *Left to right:* Penny McMorris, Nancy Crow, Ricky Clark, Clare Murray, Susan Shie. Photo courtesy FAVA archives.

Howard Fraker, Susan Harvith, Susan Hoyt, Susan Jones, Terrie Hancock Mangat, Ruth McDowell, Penny McMorris, Barbara Musser, Elaine Plogman, Chris Pritchard, Haley Pritchard, Michael Randles, John Seyfried, Robert Shaw, Susan Shie, and Charles and Ford von Weise. Special thanks to the North East Ohio Regional Quilt Council for its generous financial support of this book; the Firelands Association for the Visual Arts in Oberlin, Ohio, especially to Kyle Michalak and Betsy Manderen; Citifolk in Dayton, Ohio; Amy Bartter and Cris Rom at the Cleveland Institute of Art; the staff at Ohio University Press and senior editor Gillian Berchowitz; The Ohio Quilt Series editors Ricky Clark, Donna Sue Groves, and Ellice Ronsheim; Ron Gargasz at WBGU-TV in Bowling Green, Ohio; and Lark Publications in Asheville, North Carolina, for the use of its research library. Thank you, thank you, thank you.

Uncommon Threads

Ideal Love Mates Shrine (detail), 1985. JoAnn Giordano.
46" x 39". Color Xerox transfer, screenprint on cotton, hand-
and machine-quilted. This piece was inspired by the artist's
collection of vintage and World War II–era postcards.
Giordano says this piece, exhibited in Quilt National in 1985,
was the first one she quilted. Much of Giordano's work deals
with gender issues. The quilt is a spoof on romantic love.
Photo courtesy of the artist.

The Groundwork for a Quilt Revolution

"THE ART QUILT HAS EMERGED," PENNY McMorris and Michael Kile announced in their seminal book, *The Art Quilt*, "and it heralds a dramatic and fundamental change in the history of quilts. . . . The art quilt is different from its predecessors: it is art for walls, not beds, created by artists abandoning media like painting, printmaking and ceramics to express themselves in original designs of cloth and thread."[1]

The early pioneers of the art quilt movement began to emerge into the public eye in Ohio as the result of sweeping social, economic, and cultural changes in the decades following World War II. For the state of Ohio to give rise to an art movement that achieved international stature in just a few years might seem unlikely. Yet several historical and cultural factors converged to create the environment for this development. As pioneers settled the Ohio frontier, the diverse immigrant populations contributed to a regionalism that was enhanced by the unusual number of prominent urban centers in the state. The earliest land laws endowed Ohio with an extensive system of colleges and universities, located in both rural and urban areas throughout the state and complemented by numerous museums, art centers, and other cultural organizations that attracted Ohio's art quilt pioneers in the 1970s. Moreover, Ohio's rich quiltmaking history provided a legacy and a point of reference for Ohio's contemporary artists.

As quilt historian Roderick Kiracofe reminds us, "The history of quilts is embedded in our culture, and conversely, the history of our culture is stitched into our quilts. Understanding one sheds light on the other."[2] The end of World War II ushered in an era of drastic social, political, and economic changes. The economy, and the population, boomed following the war. A sense of national pride led to renewed interest in the arts and crafts roots of the country, and new wealth revived interest in purchasing and collecting art. Ohio had more museums in the decades leading up to the war than any other state.[3]

Many of the Ohio artists who played a role in the early years of the new quilt movement were born during or shortly after World War II and were affected by the dramatic cultural shifts occurring in the postwar era as they came of age. Those who grew up in Ohio shared the cultural knowledge of Ohio's rich quilt history, a legacy of Ohio's social and political prominence throughout the nineteenth century. While a few of these artists had been introduced to quiltmaking, almost all knew how to sew, and many of them had learned these skills from their mothers or grandmothers.

As scholars and collectors Patsy Orlofsky and the late Myron Orlofsky wrote in their landmark book, *Quilts in America*, "There has never been an interruption in the making of quilts. . . . It is one of the few handicrafts that has continued uninterrupted almost as it originally evolved."[4] From the late 1930s through the 1960s, when American quilt-making generally declined, Ohio's rural and farm women, church groups, and members of Amish and Mennonite communities continued their quilting activities.[5] Several Ohio artists would later benefit from the experience of women who preserved and valued quiltmaking during the war and postwar years. For example, Nancy Crow learned to quilt at a senior citizens' center in Cambridge, Ohio; Susan Shie's mother, raised a Mennonite, was a quilter; Wenda von Weise hosted groups of Amish quilters in her home; Terrie Hancock Mangat was influenced by Mrs. Earl B. Clay, an old-time, experienced Kentucky quiltmaker.

The end of World War II "signaled a new era for American crafts," curator Lloyd Herman observed. "New forms abounded in every medium. . . . The principal media for modern expressions were clay and fiber."[6] Returning veterans flooded the universities, and the universities began to add craft courses to meet the demand. Rose Slivka, the first editor of *Craft Horizons*, recalled, "It was a heyday for the arts as university and professional schools established workshops and provided materials on an unprecedented scale, fostering a whole new generation of artists and teachers of art."[7] While the university

Marie Snyder Shie (1917–2001) embroidering on one of daughter Susan's BFA exhibition pieces, a series of kimono shapes representing the women in her life. Marie was raised as a Mennonite in rural Wayne County; her maternal grandparents were Amish. Daughter Susan says, "Mom made traditional quilts in a very perfectionist way, and taught me to sew in that same careful, very neat and sturdy way." Photo courtesy of the artist.

programs remained focused on functional crafts in the early years, the changes taking place in the art world, including the rising number of craft conferences, forums, and magazines, gradually brought content (as opposed to function) to the forefront.

Ohio craft artists and institutions exerted broad influence throughout the twentieth century and were in the forefront of the craft movement nationwide. Easy access from rural areas to cities, cultural centers, and higher education had a positive impact on the state's artists, as the renewed interest in craft began to be reflected in university curricula. In 1965, Nancy Crow and Sue Hoyt, for example, completed their undergraduate studies in the Ohio State University ceramics program. Created in 1928 by Arthur Baggs as a supplement to the university's engineering department, the ceramics program he developed led the way to the establishment of ceramics as an art form, placing "ceramics in the same orbit as fine arts mediums and help[ing] set the stage for the rise of the studio pottery movement during the 1950s and 1960s."[8]

CLEVELAND institute of art

PROFESSIONAL TRAINING

Painting	Photography
Sculpture	Ceramics
Graphics	Weaving
Industrial Design	Textile Design
Interior Design	Silversmithing
Advertising	Enameling
Illustration	Teaching Training

DIPLOMAS · DEGREES · SCHOLARSHIPS · CATALOG ON REQUEST

Write: Director of Admissions, 11141 East Boulevard, Cleveland 6, Ohio

Cleveland Institute of Art advertisement, 1963. Promotional copy for the professional training program shows the typical areas of study available at the time.

Wenda von Weise, c. 1975, giving a silk-screening demonstration at the Cleveland Institute of Art. Photo courtesy the von Weise estate.

A casual perusal of *Craft Horizons* and *Fiberarts* magazines throughout most of the 1970s reveals no mention of quiltmaking.[9] Rather, discussions of works in fiber are focused on weaving, which had moved into the forefront of fiber aesthetics beginning in the 1950s, and also included several Ohioans among its pioneers. Before turning their attention to quiltmaking, Virginia Randles, Françoise Barnes, Elaine Plogman, Nancy Crow, David Walker, Linda Fowler, Judith Vierow, and Wenda von Weise all studied weaving.

In an atmosphere of experimentation, the first generation of postwar artists "made it up as they went along," Slivka observed.[10] The newly educated artists began to fill positions in the universities or to create entirely new departments focused on craft, such as the ones at Ohio University, Kent State University, Miami University, and the Cleveland Institute of Art. Ohio fiber artists such as Wenda von Weise, JoAnn Giordano, Petra Soesemann, and Clare Murray, like artists in other media, all taught within the university system, passing their extensive knowledge and experience on to the next generation.

The Whitney Exhibition: Quilts Return to the Public Eye

In 1971, a seminal exhibition of quilts from the early twentieth century, called Abstract Design in American Quilts, was held at the Whitney Museum of American Art in New York. Prior to this exhibition, with the exception of a few museums that presented rare exhibitions, quilts were not yet being widely collected, nor did they enjoy art status. Before World War II, a few museums had the foresight to add quilts to their textile collections. In the late 1950s, the Shelburne Museum in Vermont began showing quilts on walls. Former Shelburne curator Robert Shaw notes that the museum's founder, Electra Havemeyer Webb, "was one of the first people who thought about and presented quilts as works of art."[11]

The Whitney show is commonly considered to be the turning point in the recognition of quilts as art. Collectors Jonathan Holstein and Gail van der Hoof selected the pieces shown strictly for their strength of design and visual appeal. In a *New York Times* article written just before the exhibition opened, Holstein was interviewed: "I'd seen so many I didn't see them. . . . But then I found this horizontally striped one, dating from 1870. And I said, by God, that's what today's painting is about —that flat, spare design, the reductive sense of line and form. . . . In effect, quilt makers painted with fabrics, and we began to judge them like a body of painting."[12] At the dawn of feminism in the early 1970s, this was a new and controversial way of looking at the humble bed quilt.

The exhibition traveled around the United States and then in Europe, giving "impetus to an 'art quilt' movement around the world,"[13] and moved the art versus craft debate to the forefront. In his 1973 book *The Pieced Quilt: An American Design Tradition*, Holstein compared these quilts to paintings. "Intriguing and startling as these resemblances may be, however, any direct linking of the two mediums would be demeaning to the history and presence of both quilts and painting. . . . The women who made pieced quilts were not 'artists,' that is, they did not intend to make art, [and] had no sense of the place of their work in a continuous stream of art history."[14] In a footnote to this assertion, Holstein illustrated Robert Rauschenberg's "combine" painting *Bed* (1955), which incorporates a Log Cabin quilt, and contrasted it with quilts: "The quilt was taken from a bed, where it had no doubt served to warm sleeping householders. Were they all-unsuspecting sleeping under 'art,' or did the quilt become that only when Rauschenberg made his bed on the wall? . . . The answer would have to be that Rauschenberg made the quilt into art by incorporating it into his painting."[15] Rauschenberg's work has been recognized as an example of the crossover between artistic media representing the new freedom artists in all media found in the combination of "low" and "high" art, a trend which began in the 1950s and continues today.

Despite his contributions to the evolution of the quilt as art, Holstein was criticized by art historian and feminist writer Patricia Mainardi for his patriarchal approach. "[Holstein] has turned the innovators into the followers and used the quilts to legitimate contemporary formalist painting, while managing to dismiss these women as artists at the same time. It is an historic impossibility for art to 'mirror' . . . *forward* into time—when male artists are ahead of their time, they are called 'avant-garde.'"[16]

Quilts: The Great American Art, as advertised in *Quilter's Newsletter Magazine*. Art historian and feminist writer Patricia Mainardi confronts chauvinistic views about women's needlework in the early 1970s.

Quilter's Newsletter Magazine editor Bonnie Leman grappled with both viewpoints in her editorials. Writing about the impact of the exhibition in 1971, she exclaimed, "It seems to be official now—quiltmaking is indeed an art!"[17] In 1974 she published a paragraph from Mainardi's original article with her comments, "These remarks . . . are pertinent in the ongoing debate about whether quiltmaking is art or craft."[18]

Although the Whitney exhibition was shown in Ohio at the Akron Art Institute in 1973, of those I interviewed, only quilt historian Ricky Clark saw the original show.[19] Less important, then, for its direct influence on Ohio quilt artists in the early 1970s, the exhibition had a more direct impact on the American psyche. It caused the powerful decision makers in the art world to look at quilts in a new way, and thus enabled the public to become reacquainted with quilts and begin to consider them from a different perspective. Perhaps the greatest impact of the Whitney show was due to mass media coverage, which created a dialogue in reviews and critical writing at a time when women's work in general was being reconsidered.[20]

Outside Ohio, a few other artists were exploring the new quilt medium in the early years, often flying under the radar of the art world. California artist and author Jean Ray Laury had been making and designing quilts as early as the 1950s, and much of her early work was published in women's magazines such as *Woman's Day*. She wrote two influential books, *Appliqué Stitchery* (1966) and *Quilts and Coverlets: A Contemporary Approach* (1970).[21] Clearly anticipating the sentiment of the emerging art quilt pioneers, she wrote: "At its best, a quilt is a personal expression—not a mimic of the ideas or designs or color preferences set down by someone else."[22]

Other books were influential for Ohio's quilt artists: Beth Gutcheon's *The Perfect Patchwork Primer* (1974) and Michael James's *The Quiltmaker's Handbook: A Guide to Design and Construction* (1978), the first quilt design book aimed specifically at quilt artists. Other important resources were *Quilter's Newsletter Magazine, Fiberarts,* and the *Surface Design Journal,* periodicals that disseminated information about current exhibitions and provided early recognition and support to quilt artists.[23]

Throughout the 1950s and into the early 1960s, prosperity and a new focus on leisure gave rise to an unprecedented youth culture full of optimism. Rock and roll and television, which would become the eyes, ears, and voice for this new generation, were already affecting the culture nationwide. The space race was on, and the economy was booming.

Anything seemed possible. There were, however, dark undercurrents, which rose to the surface as the sixties progressed. The civil rights movement, as it won its first tentative victories, had been brought into national consciousness in part by the inequitable treatment of black war veterans. The internal anti-Communist paranoia embodied in McCarthyism gave way to a developing hysteria manifested in the Cold War. United States military advisers were already in Vietnam.

By the end of the sixties the optimism had dis-appeared, replaced by a deep disenchantment. The violence and upheaval at home and abroad were broadcast nightly in American living rooms. As the decade neared its end, many of the countercultural forces formed from sixties activism began to retreat, while the emerging feminist voices grew louder.

"The American Dream began to tarnish, just as the artistic sophistication and technical virtuosity of America's craft makers began to flourish," wrote Lloyd Herman and Matthew Kangas in their sur-vey of craft work from that era.[24] For the emerging new quiltmakers, the atmosphere was like no other in history, as women's work of the previous genera-tions began to be examined through the new femi-nist lens. The women's liberation movement, in part an outgrowth of the antiwar and civil rights move-ments, had, as historian Alice Echols observed, "of all the sixties movements . . . alone carried on and extended into the 1970s."[25] As a result, a growing number of alternative organizations and groups that focused on the needs of women were created. Within the increasingly popular quilting world, quilt guilds and organizations such as the National Quilting Association (established in 1969) formed in response to women's growing desire to meet and share their interests.

Susan Shie painting the *Kuan Yin Robe (for Marie Shie)*, Jan-uary 1981. BFA exhibition, the College of Wooster, artist's studio. Shie is among the few artists interviewed who were politically active during the 1970s. Befriended by feminist artist Miriam Schapiro during her artist residencies at the College of Wooster and Kent State University, Shie was en-couraged to bring her feminist voice into her artwork. She began to work first on unstretched canvas, then on un-bleached muslin, allowing her to incorporate stitching and, later, her diaristic narration into her artwork. Photo courtesy of the artist.

Feminist art by Judy Chicago and Miriam Schapiro, among others, has been linked to Latino and Black American art emerging at the same time, as "rooted in experiences of injustice and inequality that were recognized as intolerable in the 1960s."[26] The feminist movement struck various chords in the Ohio quilters interviewed. While there were certainly social and cultural influences, only two quilters felt their artwork was directly influenced by the movement. Some were turned off by what they perceived as further marginalization. Nancy Crow's comments capture what many women artists felt at the time: "Definitely in the '60s, all of us women in art school . . . were proud that there were women out there being vocal. . . . Ohio State University put up this [Judy Chicago] exhibition, *The Embroidery*

Project. . . . I just remember feeling such anger going through the exhibit about the way she was blatantly telling me about what it was like to have a baby, and she had never had a baby in her life. . . . By then, I was also starting to struggle with my own strong opinions about how I [felt] that she . . . had other women do all this work. . . . She was the so-called artist, and the rest of them are the ones who do the work. . . . Here's my bottom line feeling: If some . . . woman in the history of the world has made an apron for herself, and it's an extraordinary apron, to me it's art. . . . I don't need to put that apron in my work to make it art."[27] Crow's broad influence and strong convictions about crediting those who participate in finishing artwork for artists had led to the current convention of crediting the women who quilt the artists' quilts.

The increased interest in the handmade, already visible in the universities, was also integral to the counterculture philosophy of the late 1960s and early '70s. Those newly trained in textiles, now called "fiber artists," were graduating from university programs at a time when the economy was shrinking and there was stiff competition for university positions. Ohio quilt artists such as Nancy Crow, Terrie Hancock Mangat, Susan Shie, and James Acord, eager to supplement their incomes, made and sold ceramics and other items crafted from cloth and leather. Artists often combined cultural forces with the hippies, who embraced self-sufficiency in a back-to-the-land philosophy. The need of both groups for an outlet for their handcrafted wares and clothing created an upsurge of craft cooperatives and community craft fairs. The Woodstock movie released in 1970 shows the range of patchwork worn by both men and women: jeans, jackets, shirts, and skirts worn with patched and

A typical craft fair in the late 1960s. Photo courtesy of the FAVA archives.

embroidered bags and topped with tie-dyed T-shirts, bandanas, scarves, and vests.

Penny McMorris recalls her early exposure to the burgeoning patchwork renaissance: "I didn't notice any real patchwork in magazines until about 1968, when I saw an article I'll never forget, about a spectacular patchwork bedroom designed by Gloria Vanderbilt. . . . After I saw that room, patchwork in magazines just naturally caught my eye. . . . But it was slim pickings . . . until 1971."[28] The following year in Bowling Green, Ohio, McMorris "found a local head store . . . that wanted . . . patchwork on work shirts, so," she says, "that was the very first thing . . . I had done."[29] In Oberlin, Susan Copeland Jones had a small business creating custom patchwork clothing for a local boutique.[30] Parma artist Lois Carroll and Clare Murray of Canton spent several years early in their careers in a unique collaboration, producing wearable originals. Many artists, such as Wenda von Weise and Nancy Crow, also made patchwork clothing for their personal wardrobes.

Patchwork clothing, 1970. Susan Copeland Jones. Created to supplement her income, Jones's clothing also captured the fashion sense of the time. Image courtesy of the artist's archives and the *Oberlin News Tribune.* Photo by John Seyfried.

Patchwork Dinner Skirt, 1970. Wenda von Weise. Plastic, batik, tie-dye, bonded silver lamé. Photo courtesy the von Weise estate.

Men's Vest and Jacket, 1989. Clare Murray and Lois Carroll. The artists jointly created a line of wearables combining knitted and pieced designs by sending the work back and forth in the mail. Many of the designs incorporated Murray's hand-dyed fabrics. Photo courtesy of the artists.

Window yardage (detail), c. 1973. Wenda von Weise. Screenprint on cotton. Von Weise's early mastery of the intricacies of silk-screening fabric and her explorations of surface design techniques are evident in the raw ingredients she created for her quilts and clothing. Photo courtesy the von Weise estate.

During this same time, the surface design movement exploded onto the scene as artists explored forgotten techniques and incorporated the new technologies available to them. According to craft historians Lloyd E. Herman and Matthew Kangas, "The quilt format regained popularity among contemporary artists when the Surface Design movement offered to quilt makers such unorthodox patterning techniques as direct dyeing and painting on fabric, rubber stamping of motifs, and integration of unconventional materials and found objects."[31] Decades later, this movement is still one of the most important influences on quilt artists, as they continue to experiment with creating their own materials. The publication of numerous how-to books and the proliferation of workshops on technical aspects of surface design have made some techniques fairly commonplace today. Other techniques still in their infancy include the use of computers in combination with digital photography and of printers capable of printing large widths of fabric. These promise to have a profound impact on the fiber creations of the future.[32]

While the Whitney show had toured the country, fueling a renewed interest in quilts in certain circles, the United States bicentennial celebration

Reflections on Spring, 2003. Britt Friedman. 37" x 49". Digital print on fabric.

and associated quilt competitions inspired large numbers of experienced and novice quilters alike to create quilts. As the craze for group projects spread across the country during the bicentennial, group quilts were made to commemorate communities all over Ohio. Inspired by such a project, a postcard of the Hudson River quilt made in her hometown, in early 1974 quilt historian Ricky Clark organized a similar project. With twenty-nine other women, she oversaw the creation of the *Oberlin Quilt,* which honored the upcoming bicentennial and the sesquicentennial of Oberlin, Ohio.[33] This was the first of several Oberlin community quilting projects organized by Clark.

Meanwhile, in Maumee, Ohio, artist Judi Warren Blaydon participated with forty-two other women in the creation of the *Maumee Quilt,* beginning in 1974. Their project was focused on creating a "handmade record of residences reflecting the historical development of an Ohio River town. . . . The *Maumee Quilt* exists because a number of Maumee women shared an interest in participating jointly in a traditional American art form in celebration of the American Bicentennial."[34] Like many thousands of others, Warren Blaydon, then a painter, learned to make quilts through her involvement in a bicentennial commemorative quilt project.

Ohio Patchwork '76

In 1976, Penny McMorris mounted Ohio's first statewide traveling exhibition of contemporary quilts, Ohio Patchwork '76.[35] In retrospect, this exhibition was the point of confluence for Ohio artists already exploring quiltmaking as an art form in the 1970s. For McMorris, creating the exhibition was a fulfillment of her simple desire to see what other quilters in the state were doing. The rules of the show were simple: it was to be a juried show of quilts made in the previous three years in Ohio.

The exhibit opened in August 1976 at the Fine Art Gallery on the campus of Bowling Green State University (BGSU) and was on display for about two weeks. A slide lecture was presented during the opening. The exhibit then traveled to the State Office Tower in Columbus, the Convention Center in Dayton, and on to Cleveland. McMorris had secured funding for the exhibition and for production of a modest catalog through a National Endowment for the Arts (NEA) grant. She began to contact others she had read about in *Quilter's Newsletter Magazine*. In fact, she relied so much on that connection, she wrote a letter of frustration to editor Bonnie Leman in 1976: "When you feature the work of an individual, would it be possible to print her address so that anyone could contact her to ask if slides of her work could be purchased?"[36] The response was a negative. She did somehow manage to find Michael James in Massachusetts. "I just called

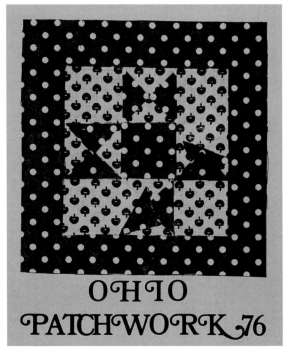

Ohio Patchwork '76 catalog. Penny McMorris says, "I had no idea how to . . . lay a catalog out, so I cut out Ohio Star patches and pasted them onto paper. The local printer dislodged one so it was crooked, and printed the cover with the lopsided quilt block. It was too late to reprint, so that's the way the cover remained." Photo by John Seyfried. Catalog courtesy of Penny McMorris.

him up and said, 'Hi, I'm interested in quilts, too.' That was how few people were doing it."[37]

Some of the works shown in Ohio Patchwork '76 were traditional and some were group bicentennial quilts, such as the *Oberlin Quilt*. Penny McMorris recalled that among them "were early works by quiltmakers who would later become among the best-known in the country," such as Nancy Crow, Françoise Barnes, Elaine Plogman, Wenda von Weise, and Judi Warren Blaydon.[38]

McMorris recalled the actual grind of traveling the show: "In reality, what it amounted to was my stuffing the quilts into my car and driving to Cleveland, Columbus, and Dayton with a daughter in tow, to put up and take down one-day exhibits so I wouldn't have to be away from home for more than one night."[39] As she explained in a later newspaper interview, "After that [exhibit], I quit quilting. . . . I realized that the reason I did the show was to see what was going on outside my immediate area. When I saw what people like Nancy Crow and . . . Wenda von Weise were doing, I was so impressed that I decided I would rather support other artists than quilt myself."[40] The connections formed as a result of the exhibition would serve McMorris well in the future, as she would go on to write, lecture, develop public television programs, and assist in forming some of the world's premiere collections of what would be called "art quilts" by everyone within a decade.[41]

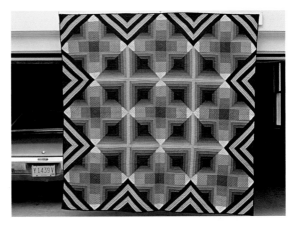

Crosses, 1976. Nancy Crow. 96" x 96". Commercial cottons/blends, machine-pieced; hand-quilted by a group of Ohio Amish women. Crow exhibited three quilts in Ohio Patchwork '76, including this one. She says, "[T]his quilt was the beginning of my being more original and it served as the basis for my three Liturgical quilts, *Incarnation, Crucifixion, Resurrection.*" Crow photographed all her quilts through 1979 hanging from her garage in Athens. She wanted the garage to be included in this image, so that readers would know that she could not afford a professional photographer in the early years. Collection Ardis and Robert James. Photo courtesy of the artist.

Elizabeth's Grandson's World, 1974. Wenda von Weise. 85" x 75". Photo silk screen with dyes on cotton, trapunto, machine- and hand-quilted. One of two quilts von Weise exhibited in Ohio Patchwork '76, this is part of a series of family quilts she made in the early 1970s. Von Weise was an early pioneer of image transfer techniques. In the catalog, Penny McMorris wrote, "These quilted pieces . . . [are] reminiscent of 19th century quilts made of souvenir handkerchiefs . . . printed with photographs." Photo courtesy the von Weise estate.

Ohio's Art Quilt Pioneers

The Beginning of a Movement

As QUILT HISTORIAN BARBARA BRACKMAN HAS observed, "It should be no surprise to quilt scholars that once the culture began interpreting antique quilts as art, we created an opportunity for liberal analysis of the artist's meaning. If today's art quilters express themselves through their quilts, we begin to assume that quiltmakers in the past used quilts as a means of expression."[1] Quiltmakers have always created original designs and, historically, quilts provided one of the few creative outlets available to the women who made them. However, these quilters were never part of a larger, identifiable movement dedicated exclusively to the creation of original designs for quilts that were never intended to function as bedcovers. This began to change in the 1970s.

By the early 1970s, both historical and contemporary quilts were being shown all over Ohio. A 1972 issue of *Quilter's Newsletter Magazine* listed eight Ohio venues in its Places to See Quilts column.[2] Although they did not travel the state as Ohio Patchwork '76 did, other exhibitions in the mid-1970s showed the work of Ohio's contemporary quiltmakers. In fact, Ohio's many regional art centers and galleries played a considerable role in bringing Ohio's quilt artists into public view. One of the earliest to begin showing such work was the Mansfield Art Center under the leadership of Daniel Butts III. Nancy Crow, Susan Shie, Elizabeth Cave, and others have credited Butts's dedication to exhibiting their work with helping launch their careers.[3] As early as January 1976, Butts curated an exhibit at the Mansfield Art Center showing the work of Françoise Barnes, Nancy Crow, and Sue Hoyt along with quilts by the West Virginia Mountain Artisans cooperative.

For Ohio artists already exploring new approaches to quiltmaking in the 1970s, such exhibitions prepared the way for the rapid expansion of quilting activity in the state. Clustered mainly around universities and other cultural institutions, still largely unknown to each other and often working in isolation, the artists began to be in touch with each other for the first time. As they became acquainted, many exchanged slides of their work, informing one another of the progress they were making. As Nancy Crow explained, "In the mid-

'70s, there were so few books on quiltmaking that most of us were self-taught. We were isolated in various sections of the United States, unaware of what others were doing. But 'something was in the air.'"4

Wenda von Weise

In the early 1960s, before the Whitney exhibition brought quilts into the consciousness of the main-stream art world, before the feminist movement reached its peak, and long before most other Ohio artists were exploring the quilt medium, Wenda (Fraker) von Weise (1943–84) was looking for her artist's voice through photography and fabric.

The only daughter and eldest of five children, Wenda was born in 1943 in Princeton, New Jersey. As her eldest son, Ford, describes it, "She was brought up in a very privileged, old, blue-blood aristocratic background from the East Coast. . . . [The idea of being an artist] was never really all that well supported. . . . She was raised to be a soci-ety wife."5 Nantucket had been her family's summer home for generations and the landscape there, like the Ohio landscape, would play a large role in the visual imagery of her artwork in years to come.

Von Weise grew up sewing, taught by her mother, a watercolorist who, as a society wife, was "never allowed to cultivate [her talent]."6 Wenda "had a long history with [fabric]. When she was a girl, with [her mother] she did crochet and needle-point, and they sewed a lot. There was always a sewing room in her house growing up. . . . She was always into fabric."7

In 1959, despite discouragement from her family (she was only seventeen), Wenda married and moved to her husband's hometown, Cincinnati, Ohio.

Encouraged by her mother-in-law, she enrolled in classes at the Cincinnati Museum of Art, where she had studied the textile and spectacular tapestry collection, donated by the von Weise family. In the early 1960s the young family moved to Gates Mills, Ohio. Wenda continued to develop her work in fiber and photography. She began what would become a lifelong project of photographing and documenting the landscapes around her, especially the nearby Kneale farm. "I first started putting photographs on fabric," she recalled, "using the photo-screenprinting process, and printing the colors using dye. . . . Once I have an image on my silk-screen there are various ways I go about using it. I know that I'm going to use it more than once since it takes a great deal of time and effort to get the image onto the screen. . . . Over a ten-year period I took hundreds and hundreds of photographs of [the Kneale] farm. . . . The first quilt, *Cornfield*, is owned by Mr. Kneale. . . . In fact, Mr. and Mrs. Kneale quilted it after I had printed it."8

In 1969, Wenda von Weise and her close friend Donna van Dijk enrolled in the fibers program at the Cleveland Institute of Art (CIA). Because they both had two young sons, they negotiated the creation of self-directed, part-time study programs at CIA. Ford von Weise recalls that his father was not supportive of the CIA classes, because Wenda was a young mother with a family to raise. In an interview shortly before her death, von Weise re-called, "When I was with young children at home, there was a void. I was doing a lot of volunteer work, but somehow that wasn't fulfilling enough for me, so I went to school, because I had this great need. . . . I was very fortunate to be able to afford to have [a nanny]. . . . Thanks to her, I was able to finish school."9

Ralph Kneale quilting the *Kneale Cornfield Quilt*, c. 1977. Wenda von Weise. 91" x 81". Photo screenprint on cotton. Hand-quilted. Von Weise enjoyed the interaction of allowing others to participate in quilting her artwork. Here, the late Ralph Kneale quilts on the images of his farm. Von Weise presented the quilt to the Kneales as a gift. Photo courtesy the von Weise estate.

CIA's fiber program, like most in the United States at that time, was heavily focused on industrial design, weaving and textile design being the primary areas of study. Von Weise majored in textile design with a minor in photography. Her studies coincided with the rumblings of change in the art world, the wide cross-exploration of media by her contemporaries, and the mounting visibility of the craft movement.

Although she had extensive sewing experience, von Weise was drawn to making quilts for aesthetic reasons: "The idea of the family photograph album and its history; the idea of the family quilt and how so many quilts were prized and treasured and kept away. I wanted to combine both of them, so I learned the photographic techniques I needed to know [in order to] transfer the photographic im-

ages to the fabric and to quilt them." She borrowed all the old family photos and worked through an entire series of quilts until, as she put it, "I had said what I wanted to say."[10]

In the early 1970s, von Weise had the opportunity to study with Robert Rauschenberg, who was already well known for his experimental "combines," and was also a highly regarded printmaker.[11] Because of her interest in photography, silk-screen techniques, and printing of imagery on fabric, von Weise's work with Rauschenberg greatly informed her development. She brought the techniques she had learned from Rauschenberg back to Cleveland, and later, to CIA. According to her son, "She was the only person doing it in Cleveland at that time. . . . She had to set it all up, [and] did it all [initially] off campus."[12]

In 1975, von Weise completed her BFA at the art institute and won a scholarship to attend graduate school. That same spring, she won a prize at the Cleveland Museum of Art's May Show, and the museum bought the piece.[13] By 1976, she already had wide contacts in the national art world, including gallery representation in New York. She had already had a one-woman show in Cleveland, and her work was included in the New York exhibition The New American Quilt, which quilt expert Robert Shaw describes as "the first major museum exhibition of non-traditional quilts."[14] Von Weise's work was shown along with pioneering fiber artists such as Gwen-lin Goo, Susan Hoffman, Molly Upton, Gayle Fraas and Duncan Slade, M. Joan Lintault, Katherine Westphal, and Lenore Davis.[15] In the catalog, curator Ruth Amdur Tanenhaus wrote, "The artists represented in this exhibition have transcended the historical quilt form by utilizing novel treatments to realize fresh images in fiber. . . . These contemporary examples of a traditional American craft place form over function."[16]

Determined to continue her education, for graduate studies, von Weise chose Cranbrook Academy in Bloomfield Hills, Michigan, commuting from Gates Mills. She enrolled in the fiber program and studied with Gerhardt Knodel, completing her MFA in 1978.[17] In her master's thesis, she discussed the relationship between quiltmaking and photography in her artwork. "There are certain aspects of photography that are inherent in the medium itself and are important considerations in my exploration of photo imagery in quilt making. . . . The easy duplication and repetition of photographs . . . is the most important connection between photography and quilt making."[18]

In the late 1970s, von Weise's drive to be an artist sounded the death knell for an already struggling marriage. She moved to urban Cleveland Heights after her divorce and taught part-time until securing a full-time teaching position at CIA when Gwen-lin Goo's departure created an opening in the fiber department. At home, she kept her sewing, quilting, and weaving equipment in one room and set up her photographic studio and darkroom in an unventilated basement. In the early 1980s, she was diagnosed with lung cancer.

Her final series of work, the Fabricated Landscape and Dreamscape series, explored landscape related to her ongoing environmental concerns. In an interview televised a few months before her death, von Weise discussed this series: "Some of the organizational ideas in those quilts ranged around Rauschenberg's idea of the random image, what he called the 'vernacular glance.' I was tying that idea up with the idea of surrealist imagery . . . the double image, the image printed randomly, upside down,

Wenda von Weise defending her BFA exhibition, 1975. Cleveland Institute of Art. One of von Weise's exhibition quilts, *Dream Quilt: Nantucket Film Strip* (1975, 112" x 90"), hangs behind her. This piece illustrates her beginning explorations of landscape, presented in a grid format. Photo courtesy the von Weise estate.

flipped over, overprinted . . . the idea that dreams occur in bed, and quilts, of course, fit on a bed."[19] This functional aspect of her work was important to her.

Despite her technically focused approach to construction, von Weise's work was primarily about a sense of place. "Her art was extraordinarily influenced by being in Ohio. . . . She was always an Ohio artist, which was cemented by the fact that most of her quilts were quilted by the Amish. . . . She found a connection to the culture and to the landscape through her art by doing that."[20]

In the summer of 1984, she taught at the Haystack School in Maine, accompanied by her soul-mate and fellow artist, her brother, Howard. Her death that fall was an abrupt end to a promising career and a great loss to the community of artists. Fortunately, she left a legacy of work in private collections and in her family's personal collections.

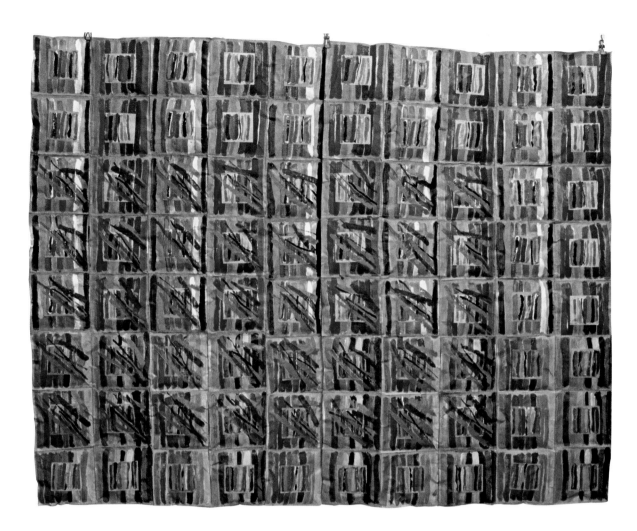

Mirjana Ugrinov

An immigrant to Cleveland in 1970, Mirjana Ugrinov was born in the former Yugoslavia in 1950 and grew up in a region where needlework was revered. From Ugrinov's earliest memories, her creative grandmother bought her paper and colored pencils, thereby encouraging Ugrinov's lifelong desire to be an artist. After studying painting at Ohio State University for two years, she completed her degree at Kent State University. Ugrinov credits a painting instructor there with her early interest in working with fibers. She saved a paper bag from a class exercise; finding it in her journal a few years later, in the mid-1970s, she began to experiment with making quilts from paper.

In the late 1970s, Ugrinov opened an art gallery in Cleveland Heights, Ohio. This enabled her to meet and provide exhibition opportunities to a wide variety of artists from the region and around the state. She also served as program director for the New Organization for the Visual Arts (NOVA), a now defunct Cleveland arts organization that supported regional artists. Ugrinov became acquainted with Wenda von Weise at NOVA when von Weise was invited to present a program.

After thirty years in Cleveland, Ugrinov moved to Chicago, where she continues to work in various media: painting, collage, ceramics, and paper constructions. "The essence of my attraction to quilts," she says, "somehow goes to the idea of quilts being so unpretentious. They're almost like the shy aspect of art."[21] At a recent symposium held in conjunction with the exhibition Ohio Pioneers of the Art Quilt, Ugrinov recalled a conversation in which Nancy Crow told her, "When they had the first Quilt National [in 1979] and saw my work, they didn't know what to do with it. . . . I was using paper grocery bags stamped on the back with names of stores."[22] By exhibiting her innovative stitched paper constructions inspired by traditional quilts in arenas such as the May Show and Quilt National, Ugrinov has helped stretch the somewhat rigid boundaries of the medium. In her work we find the pioneering groundwork for explorations by many of today's emerging artists. Despite working outside the mainstream of the quilting world, Ugrinov has produced a body of work that is representative of the pervasive influence of quilts.

Paper Quilt #12, 1983. Mirjana Ugrinov. 56" x 70". Acrylic paint and ink on rice paper, photo transfers, machine-appliquéd and machine-quilted. Photo by Marianne Pojman.

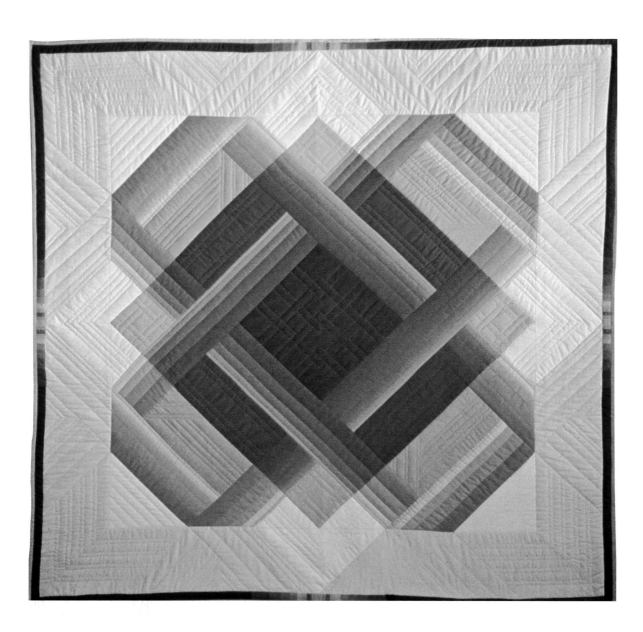

Judi Warren Blaydon

In the fall of 1976, Judi Warren Blaydon began teaching a series of quiltmaking classes called The Great American Quilt through the Adult Education Program at the Toledo Museum of Art. "I was literally one step ahead of my students," she recalls. "I taught as though it was an art class: study the history, work on design, approach the particular construction problems that design presented. These were 'first quilts' that were original designs. I was thrilled."[23] Eventually, art majors who attended her classes received undergraduate credit.

Born in 1937 in Detroit, Michigan, Judi Warren Blaydon completed an undergraduate degree in art education at Eastern Michigan University. Before she moved to Maumee, Ohio, in 1968, she had already shown her paintings at the Detroit Museum of Art.[24] Judi's paternal grandmother was the keeper of the family quilts, and was also a quiltmaker. Warren Blaydon remembers, "She bought fabrics at J. L. Hudson's in Detroit specifically for quilts, and then made housedresses with the 'leftovers.' . . . She pieced [her quilts] on a Singer sewing machine and had a quilt frame on the dining room table . . . grudgingly taking it away only to clear the table for Thanksgiving dinner!"[25] Her grandmother lived nearby when she was a child. "She did teach me a little about using a sewing

machine . . . . More importantly, she conveyed her abiding love for quilts and cloth and color."[26]

Warren Blaydon learned to quilt while working on the *Maumee Quilt,* but her transition from painting to making art quilts came by way of her grandmother. "My first paintings were quiltlike, divided into grids, with traditional American quilt compositions onto which I painted little stems and flowers. One day, while I was painting a nine-block pattern at the kitchen counter, my grandmother walked in one door of the kitchen and out the other. In passing, she said, 'If you like them so much, why don't you make a real one?'"[27] Her grandmother's influence stayed with her over the years. In a letter to the attendees of the first Art Quilt Network meeting in 1987, she wrote about why she continued to make quilts: "Because of color, because of pattern, because I watched my grandmother run her hands over her grandmother's quilts as though she was touching her, and I realized how important a vehicle quilts are for communicating, for women to speak unspoken words to each other."[28]

By 1978, more than sixty women had participated in Warren Blaydon's classes. The Toledo Museum of Art held the first of several exhibitions of their works in the winter of 1978, showing eleven quilts. The museum's press release described the exhibition: "While some quilts bear a similarity to traditional patterns, others are original and all were arrived at through a combination of experimentation, a growing understanding of the design history involved, and an eagerness to discover and make choices which were personally rewarding."[29] Classes such as the ones presented by Warren Blaydon and the other art quilt pioneers disseminated quilt design approaches and the artists' styles regionally and, in time, internationally.

Hot Möbius, 1980. Judi Warren Blaydon. 71" x 71". Tinted and bleached cotton, machine-pieced, hand-quilted. This early geometric work was inspired by the Möbius strip of German mathematician Alfred Möbius. The bands of intertwined colors move from intense to pale as they emerge from and return to the center of the composition. This piece won the Merit Award at Quilt National '81. Photo by John Kluesner.

Judi Warren Blaydon with Japanese students, 1990. Show and Tell in Judi's backyard (with translation by Atsuko Hashiura). Judi recalls, "Twenty-seven Tokyo quiltmakers came to lunch at my house on the way to Paducah. They also visited the Wolcott House in Maumee, the Maumee Bicentennial Quilt hanging in the City Hall, and The Quilt Foundry in Maumee." Photo courtesy of the artist.

Although she was politically active during the 1960s and 1970s, Warren Blaydon's artwork was most strongly influenced by her travels related to her teaching, especially her trips to Japan.[30] "I was one of six American quilters who went to Japan to teach at the First American Quilt Symposium in Japan in March of 1986. . . . I was fortunate to be invited back to teach [there] six different times between 1986 and 1993. . . . It *did* influence my work. . . . I wanted to remember every minute, every new place and sight—and I wanted to record what I saw and loved."[31]

In 1986, Warren Blaydon completed an MFA degree in printmaking and textiles at the School of Art at Bowling Green State University, "maybe the first MFA earned for making quilts! We sort of made it up as we went along . . . printing my own yardage and then using it in quilts to build a thesis exhibition for 1986."[32] By this time, Warren was al-

ready well known as an artist and a teacher. In 1994 she published her first book, *Fabric Postcards: Landmarks and Landscapes, Monuments and Meadows,* inspired by a fascination with antique postcards and their evocation of fantastic journeys. Her fabric postcards, which she describes as "quilts to be held in your hand,"[33] are representative of the trend that began in the 1980s toward smaller, more intimate, and more salable artwork.

Warren Blaydon's work, like von Weise's, evokes a strong sense of place in a dreamlike manner. With the occasional and subtle use of hand-dyed, painted, or printed fabric, Warren creates what Robert Shaw calls "atmospheric quilts based on moods and images."[34] Describing her own work, Warren Blaydon states, "Working with hand-dyed colors is somewhat like painting, and the quilting creates subtleties much the same as embellishments in a drawing."[35] Like the other pioneers of the art quilt, Warren Blaydon succeeds in large part because of her dedication: "I do what I do the way I do it because that is the only way I can do it, and because I have to do it. . . . Do the best that you can and as fast as you can. The quilts in my head don't count, as they are always wonderful."[36]

March 28, 1986: Rain at Fushimi Inari, 1988. Judi Warren Blaydon. 88" x 72". Machine-pieced and strip-pieced cotton, lamé, hand-painted and printed cotton, Skydyes, embellished with beads and cloth Omikuji knots, hand-appliquéd and quilted. Recording the memory of a rainy spring day at the Fushimi Inari Shrine, Kyoto, Japan, the artist explains: "Because this quilt is about a place I cannot forget, one paper fortune is embroidered with the words NIHON NI MATA KAERITAI: Return again to Japan." Photo by Brian Blauser.

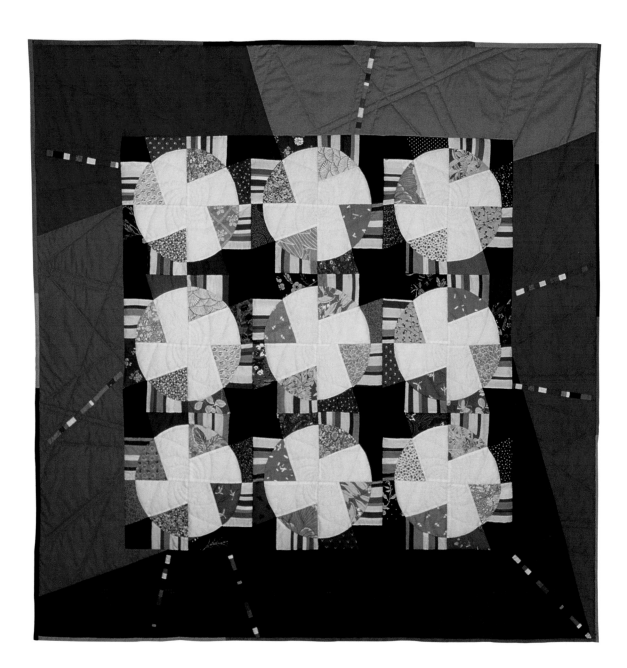

Elaine Plogman

The eldest of four children and the only daughter, Elaine (Hunighake) Plogman was born in Cincinnati, Ohio, on December 7, 1938. Located in the southwestern corner of the state on the Ohio River, Cincinnati still reflects its German ethnic roots. Separated from Kentucky only by the river, the city also reflects a unique connection to southern culture. Elaine's family has deep roots in the Cincinnati area, where her German grandfather had a grocery store and her Irish-descended mother's farm home in nearby Fayetteville was a favorite location for Sunday dinner. Elaine's mother was not a quilter, but she did piecework sewing at home, sewed curtains and dresses, and made clothing for the family's ten children. Elaine credits her mother for her early interest in sewing and her love of fabric.

Plogman received her BFA in 1960, attending a local commuter college while living at home. She recently reminisced about her college years: "We didn't have any major goals in college, other than just to get through. We felt that we were very lucky to be there. We just studied like crazy."[37] Some of her classes touched on batik and fabric design, but she began weaving on her own.[38] Although she held onto her loom until just a few years ago, like many of her contemporaries, she eventually lost interest in weaving, finding it so technically demanding to set up the loom. Before she married, she worked for three years as a display artist in a local department store. "As things happened in those days," she recalls, "what was typical was that once you were married and had a family you would stop working. That was the expectation." Her first son was born in 1964, and she left her job to care for him.

Like most of her contemporaries in urban settings, Plogman belonged to several organizations, allowing her to connect with other artists in her region. She remembers seeing a notice in the newsletter of the Craft Guild of Greater Cincinnati requesting entries for the Ohio Patchwork '76 exhibition, and later for the first Quilt National, held in 1979. The Greater Cincinnati Weaver's Guild, which she joined in the 1960s and is still affiliated with, had small interest groups. Already pursuing her interest in fabric piecing, Plogman joined the small stitchery interest group, where she met her like-minded friend Carolyn Muller, an early participant in the art quilt movement, who switched to painting in the 1980s.

The periodicals of the time were an important resource for Plogman, as they were for many of the pioneers. She remembers beginning to see quilts in magazines before the U.S. bicentennial. She was an early subscriber to *Quilter's Newsletter Magazine* and *Fiberarts:* "*Fiberarts* was . . . the first one for artwork, not traditional quilts. I got it when it was a newspaper format. Sometimes it looked like they had pasted it up with scotch tape. It's amazing that it has lasted that many years."

In the early 1970s, Plogman first saw Nancy Crow's work in a local quilt show sponsored by the

Nine Sunny Days, 1983. Elaine Plogman. 63" x 63". Cotton scraps, machine-pieced, hand-quilted. Featured in a 1984 *Quilter's Newsletter Magazine* article, Plogman discussed the important heritage of scrap quilts, and added that "it may be precisely this use of scrap fabric that is responsible for quilt-making's failure to be recognized by the world at large as a true art form." Even in her earliest work, such as this piece, Plogman's goal was to create compositions full of movement. Photo courtesy of the artist.

Sketchbook pages. Elaine Plogman. Like many artists, Plogman works out her ideas in sketches. Photo courtesy of the artist.

Cincinnati-based batting company Stearns and Foster. "I took pictures [because] I had to give a talk to somebody or other, and I needed to get some slides. . . . I wrote to Nancy and asked if I could [use the slides of her work]." When describing the early years of the art quilt movement, Plogman emphasizes how important the trading of slides was in seeing others' new work and maintaining connections. "You hadn't made enough quilts to fill an hour [lecture]. You had to get some from someplace, so everybody traded slides back and forth. . . . It kept you in touch with those people, and you knew what they were doing . . . and they'd say 'Do you want me to pay for these, or would you like slides in return?' Well, you always took slides in return."

Around this time she was already creating small unquilted wallhangings, which she describes as "little design projects." One of her earliest was exhibited in Ohio Patchwork '76. She recalls going to Bowling Green to see the show: "I just couldn't believe it. I didn't know that things like that were going on." Amid the strange mixture of quilts in the exhibit, some very traditional, she recalls others that stuck out in her mind. "Wenda von Weise's silk-screened images were so radical for that time. . . . I didn't know what to make of those."

Elaine Plogman has never followed trends, but continues to do the work she is inspired to create. "I still like to work in modular units of some kind. . . . I like to do piecing. . . . My things are known for that. . . . People tell me they can usually pick out my work by the combinations of fabric and the colors." When asked how she would like to be remembered in the future, she said, "I'm interested mainly in decorative art. I'll come right out and admit it. I really don't care to make something pictorial. I really don't care to make something with a real message in it. I just want something that's fun to make and to look at. You get a piece where all the parts come together well, and the fabrics look good together, and you have a pleasant thing to live with. . . . That satisfied me."

African Crosses (detail), 1996. Elaine Plogman. 63" x 63". Cotton, blends and rayon, block-printed, airbrushed, machine-pieced and quilted. In this richly layered work, Elaine Plogman utilized a block print made by her husband, Robert, to emphasize the crosses formed by the juxtaposition of blocks in her composition. Photo courtesy of the artist.

Terrie Hancock Mangat

Living across the river from Cincinnati in north-western Kentucky, several artists maintained such close contact with their Ohio counterparts—even keeping studios in Cincinnati—that they have traditionally been considered a part of the Ohio quiltmaking scene.[39] One of these artists is Terrie Hancock Mangat, born in 1948 and raised about ten miles from Cincinnati, in Cold Spring, Kentucky. Her parents, both born in Kentucky, met in Cincinnati, where both families had warehouses along the riverfront. Growing up, Terrie spent a lot of time with both sets of grandparents in Cincinnati. As Terrie says, "Cincinnati spans the river."[40]

Like Elaine Plogman, Terrie Mangat is descended from the German immigrants who settled Cincinnati, but her life was most affected by growing up in a region that straddles the Mason-Dixon Line, a unique area with a mix of southern and midwestern cultural and educational influences. Mangat feels that being exposed to the region's quiltmaking heritage while she was growing up "formed her technical and aesthetic foundations for quiltmaking."[41]

Although she remembers only one family quilt, a butterfly pattern, Terrie began collecting fabric as a little girl. "I asked for fabric for Christmas when I was six years old. . . . When I was five I took crayons and I started drawing fabric designs on a white sheet, and cut it out and made a doll dress for my doll." Her interest in sewing continued as she grew.

Because her mother did not sew, Terrie was sent to Singer sewing lessons when she was eleven.

Mangat studied art at the University of Kentucky, focusing on ceramics and printmaking, and received her degree in 1970. Outside the course of her regular art studies, she took a textile class in the Home Economics Department and another with a professor who taught embroidery and rug-hooking. She studied at Penland School on a summer scholarship, and learned to weave. She also took some classes at the William E. Gebhardt School of Art in Cincinnati.

Mangat was politically active throughout her college years, participating in antiwar demonstrations on campus. Married in 1970, after college, she was the family's breadwinner while her husband was still in medical school. She says, "I got a job teaching art . . . and I remember protesting, because the men could wear pants and the women couldn't. . . . The first year I taught there, my salary was $2,800."[42]

Mangat's interest in making quilts began, she says, when she saw some "amazing traditional Kentucky quilts" owned by her friend Susan. "She got these tops from a woman named Mrs. Earl Clay who lived in Carlisle, Kentucky, so I . . . bought some tops from her for $25. . . . What made me want to make quilts was how she put fabric together. . . . She broke all the rules. . . . She used men's underwear fabric from the local boxer shorts factory." Mangat maintained a lifelong friendship with Mrs. Clay, but did not learn quiltmaking from her. Relying on her existing sewing skills, along with her already substantial fabric stash, she began with reverse appliqué: "I just looked at molas and figured out how to do it." During those early years, she also made pottery, which she sold at the Berea Arts and Crafts Fair, to supplement the family income. She remembers making what she called "transition work," early mixed media pieces, boxes made of clay, drilled, and topped with a quilted piece.

By the time Mangat moved to Oklahoma City in the 1970s, she had already made many quilts, including *Giraffes,* which would appear in her first exhibition, the first Quilt National in 1979. It was in Oklahoma that Terrie met Martha Ellen Green, who she feels influenced her quiltmaking. "She used to do a lot of textile pieces, and she embellished and embroidered. . . . I was resistant to that. . . . I didn't start embellishing 'til after I left Oklahoma City. . . . I was the first one to embellish [on quilts], but it sort of absorbed into my system from Martha."

When an artist friend saw her quilts, she persuaded Terrie to submit an entry for a commission for the Alfred P. Murrah Federal Building. Mangat won the commission in 1978, and created *Oklahoma Quilt,* which "was dedicated by Mrs. Walter Mondale at the Federal Building where it hangs as the only quilt among 30 pieces of original art."[43]

Back in Cincinnati, Mangat continued to develop her pioneering whimsical style, blending Americana and folk art kitsch with narrative mixed media and highly engaging embellished compositions. In the early 1990s, after a series of emotional losses, Terrie turned to her sister, Becky. "I couldn't stand staying in my studio and being alone. I said, 'Becky, let's just open a little fabric and bead store.'" This conversation marked the birth of one of Ohio's greatest places to buy unusual fabrics, St. Theresa

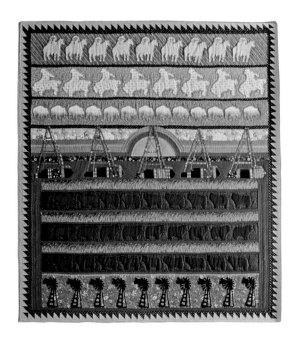

Oklahoma Quilt, 1979. Terrie Hancock Mangat. 86" x 96". Collection of the Alfred P. Murrah Federal Building, Oklahoma City, Oklahoma. Photo courtesy of the artist.

Textile Trove, which is located near Mangat's former studio, Over-the-Rhine, in inner-city Cincinnati. "The store [is] not only a commercial enterprise, but an intersection of art, culture and service. . . . Terrie created after-school programs for latch-key children, providing an alternative to the perils of the street."[44]

It is chilling to read the accounts of Mangat's Oklahoma City commission, knowing the fate of the Alfred P. Murrah Federal Building. After the bombing tragedy in 1995, Eve De Bona organized an exhibition of quilts created by many of America's leading artists in memory of the nineteen children who were killed. The exhibit Sewing Comfort out of Grief: The Oklahoma City Children's Memorial Art Quilts opened in Oklahoma City on April 19, 1996, the first anniversary of the bomb blast, and traveled across the United States for three years. Not only did Mangat's commissioned quilt survive the blast, but she created a second quilt, *Children's Casket Map,* for this exhibit. To create her map of death, Mangat thought about the pain the parents experienced and the pain she heard in the stories of violence from the inner-city children she had worked with in Cincinnati after her return there in 1980.[45]

Terrie Mangat moved full-time to her beloved Taos, New Mexico, in 1994. With a larger studio space, she has now returned to creating silk-screened fabrics in addition to quiltmaking, and has created a line of commercial fabrics. When working on a very large commission, Terrie says, she still works on the floor sometimes, but remembers that it was Nancy Crow who encouraged her to begin working on the wall. In summing up her career, Terrie spoke of Penny McMorris: "Penny was one of the most important people in my career as a quiltmaker. . . . She championed my work."

Children's Casket Map, 1996. Terrie Hancock Mangat. Cotton, acrylic paint, machine-embroidered caskets by Jan Engler, hand reverse appliquéd and hand-tied, machine-quilted. The artist says, "The FBI sent me an 87-page printout of statistics on children killed in each state in 1994. . . . I was unable to fit all the deaths into some states, so I used caskets only for children up to age 12 and listed the children killed between the ages of 13 and 18 in the map legend." Photo courtesy of the artist.

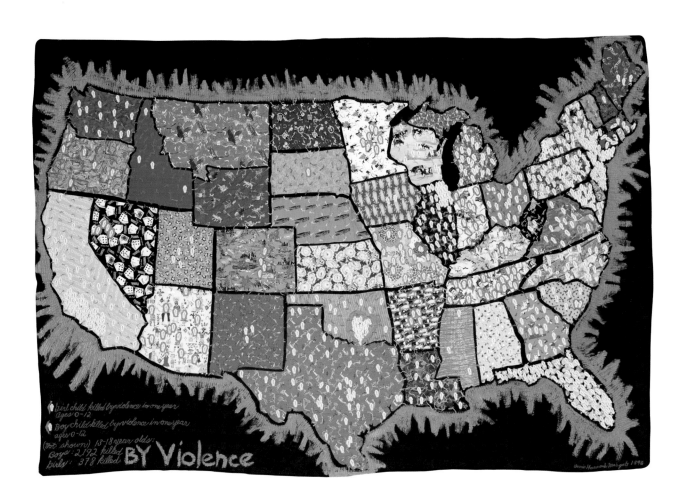

◗ Girl child killed by violence in one year
   ages 0-12
◗ Boy child killed by violence in one year
   ages 0-12
(not shown) 13-18 year olds:
Boys: 2,192 killed
Girls: 378 killed BY Violence

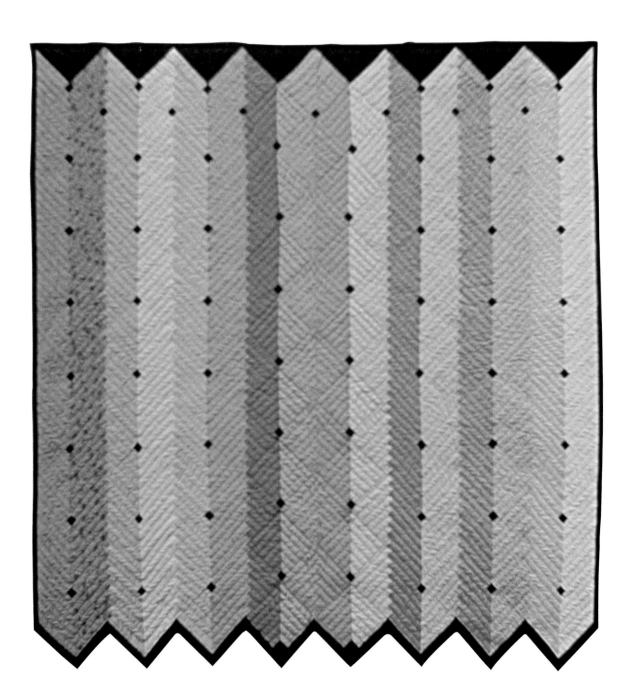

Virginia Randles

Meeting Virginia Randles in the 1980s was like encountering a favorite grandmother, but with a twist. A willing mentor, she was soft-spoken and kind, full of gentle encouragement; Virginia's exterior hid, as her son Michael describes it, "achievement through dedication to principles and perseverance in the face of adversity."[46] Alongside such diverse artistic influences as Jungian psychology and the color theory of Joseph Albers, Randles's "early fascination with her grandmother's 'button box' . . . reveals a deep inspiration which encompasses her intellectual interest in color as well as the emotional comforts we all associate with hand made quilts."[47]

Born in Sedalia, Missouri, in 1912, Virginia moved with her mother and sisters to Kansas City after her father deserted the family. She carried this experience throughout her life and translated it into a deep sense of devotion and obligation to her own family, a commitment which, in turn, carried her through the many difficult times of her life. Coming of age in the Depression and remarkably intelligent, Virginia was determined to get an education, and graduated from the University of Kansas in 1936, then earned a scholarship in medical technol-

Virginia Mae Scotten, c. 1932. A young woman during the Depression, Virginia Mae Scotten Randles was determined to make something of her life. Photo courtesy Michael Randles.

Fences, 1979. Virginia Randles. 78" x 82". Cotton/polyester broadcloth, hand-quilted by Bertha Mast. The visual inspiration for this quilt, constructed using a log cabin technique, was a palm tree at the Franklin Park Conservatory. In Randles's notes, she wrote, "Was named in deference to Robert Frost. The log cabin quilt is given the three-dimensional effect by alternating lighter and darker blocks in earthy tones of composite colors." Photo courtesy Michael Randles.

ogy at the University's School of Medicine. In an interview, Virginia said, "It was my grandmother who inspired me. . . . She . . . studied practical nursing. It was her books and her 'doctoring' that caught my attention."[48]

In the medical program Virginia met Leland Randles, whom she married in 1938. In the early 1940s, they settled in Fort Scott, Kansas, where their three children were raised. While he served as a flight surgeon in World War II, Virginia worked as a medical technologist.

After the war, in the 1950s, her son says that she was dissatisfied with her role as the "doctor's wife" in a small town. Seeking an outlet, she took up interior decoration and learned to oil paint, make

braided rugs, and weave. In the mid-1960s, Virginia and Leland moved to Athens, Ohio. The move was the beginning of her blossoming as an artist. No longer isolated, she began to connect with other women artists through organizations such as those in the Textile Arts Guild in Athens and Ohio Designer Craftsmen (ODC), headquartered in Columbus.

From the mid-1970s, when she turned away from weaving and took up quiltmaking, Randles was entirely "devoted . . . to designing and making contemporary quilts."[49] She wrote, "I have had a life-long interest in color and a desire to communicate in a non-verbal way. My quilts are intended to express aesthetically my experience and inspirations."[50] Randles recalled, "It was Nancy [Crow] who taught me to think of myself as an artist. . . . We were in the first Winterfair '77 . . . and I worked with her in organizing the first Quilt National '79."[51] One of her favorite pieces, *Fences,* was juried into the first Quilt National exhibition in 1979. Her work was exhibited that same year at the ODC show at the Columbus Cultural Arts Center and appeared in numerous books and catalogs.

In 1980, Virginia Randles bought a small house in Athens to use as a studio, and entered her most productive years. She said, "It enabled me to get my thoughts together, to give undivided attention to the work at hand, and time to call my own."[52]

By the late 1980s, Randles began to experience vision problems, and had surgery for cataracts. In the early 1990s, she moved back to Lawrence, Kansas. She was soon diagnosed with lung cancer, and, although she continued to work, she never felt well enough again to complete any new work. She died in Lawrence in March 1996. When asked how his mother might wish to be remembered, Michael Randles replied, "As her own person . . . because most of her life she got feedback from other people that she was Mrs. Leland Randles. I think that she was determined to be her own person, and be Virginia Mae Scotten Randles."[53]

Geometric mathematical relationships with shapes and a scientific approach to color use are the hallmarks of Randles's quilts. She was an early proponent of exploring color gradations and illusions of dimensionality. Breaking out of the confines of the traditionally square or rectangular, she often created shaped quilts, consistent with her vision. Aside from these contributions, Virginia Randles was an early and active member of the Art Quilt Network (AQN), formed by Nancy Crow and Columbus artist Linda Fowler in 1987, where her determination and work ethic were an inspiration to all.

Helix II, 1984. Virginia Randles. 52" round. Machine-pieced cotton, hand-quilted by Mrs. Owen Miller. Complex geometric construction techniques and a love of color were Randles's trademarks. She often created symmetrically shaped compositions, such as this one, allowing her careful color use to move the viewer's eye through the design. Photo by Leland Randles.

Sue Allen Hoyt and Françoise Barnes

Sue Allen Hoyt, born in Mount Vernon, Ohio, in 1942, began sewing when she was six. She says she "actually learned to quilt correctly from Nancy Crow's old friends in Cambridge."[54] She stopped making quilts in the 1980s, primarily because of rheumatoid arthritis, but she fondly remembers the early years in Athens. "When Nancy [Crow] and Françoise [Barnes] and Virginia [Randles] and I had our weekly 'bee' . . . we got to see (and quilt) each others' work. . . . We were really in the vanguard when we began making quilts, and there were no books on contemporary quiltmaking until a few years later." Sue also remembers the early influence of strip-piecing methods on the group: "[W]hen I made *Takht-I-Suleiman* . . . I cut strips individually and put the shapes together. It was sort of whopper-jawed when it was all assembled because the short strips were difficult to sew into a clean shape. When Nancy and Françoise saw it, they liked the idea, and they figured out that if the strips were cut longer and pieced together before the shape was cut, it could be cut out more cleanly. We tried it, it worked, and we all became strippers."

Born in Corsica and educated in France, Françoise (Guiderdoni) Barnes "has become an

Sue Hoyt and Françoise Barnes, April 1975. This image appeared in the *Athens Messenger* under the heading "Workshop Planned: Quilting Group Will Share Its Talents." Photo courtesy *The Messenger*, Athens, Ohio.

Untitled, 1982. Françoise Barnes. 80" x 80". Machine-pieced and appliquéd cotton and blends; hand-quilted. This is an early example of Barnes's exquisite use of color, symmetry, and the curved piecing she is known for. In the Quilt National '83 catalog, Barnes reveals that this piece was inspired by the photography of Malcolm Kirk in the book *Man as Art.*

Ohioan and has adopted a typically American art form to express her ideas. Quiltmaking attracted her because, 'it seemed that no one had consciously decided to push this medium as far as it could go.'"[55] Françoise came to the United States in 1967, married and settled in Athens, Ohio. Also a part of the textile guild there, she, like her friends Virginia Randles, Sue Allen Hoyt and Nancy Crow, began making quilts in the mid-1970s. Hoyt recalled, "At first I was alone, but I got to know Françoise . . . whose husband also taught at OU [Ohio University]. Nancy Crow and I were friends in grad school at OSU [Ohio State University]. . . . After she and her husband . . . moved to Athens from Cambridge . . . the three of us jumped into quilting wholeheartedly. Pretty soon we were joined by Virginia Randles."

From the earliest years of her childhood, Françoise Barnes was fascinated with the natural world, especially insects and flowers. This interest was reflected in her best-known quilts, often enlarged, abstracted symmetrical and colorful views of insects or plants, inspired by her travels to West Africa. In addition to her unique use of color, she was an early pioneer of curved piecing techniques, which she accomplished by machine, a technique she demonstrated on Penny McMorris's PBS series, *Quilting II*.[56]

In the 1980s, she resumed drawing and painting, and made her last work as a quiltmaker in the late 1980s. She said, "I had been frustrated with the obvious limitations of fabrics and I was irresistibly attracted by the immediacy and directness of painting. . . . I made the decision to desert my familiar universe."[57] Now living in Albuquerque, New Mexico, Barnes continues to create paintings incorporating collage and fabric.

Of the first Quilt National, Barnes wrote, "[I]n 1979 Nancy Crow and I decided that it was time for contemporary quiltmakers . . . to be seen and acknowledged. With the help of many others, we started Quilt National . . . the first showcase of its kind and still the pinnacle for art quiltmakers."[58] For the 1979 exhibition, the first of the biannual shows, Barnes, like Virginia Randles in 1981, donated a raffle quilt to assist in raising money to help pay the expenses of the exhibition.[59]

[In the 1970s] I was very caught up with commercial prints still. That's what I wanted to work with, and restructure them. We used to drive up to Ashland, Ohio, because there was an upholstery shop there that, for some reason, had this gigantic collection of drapery fabrics. We were trying desperately to find geometric shapes that could be cut up and restructured, because you couldn't find anything like that in a regular fabric shop. There weren't quilt shops then. Linda Fowler and I used to drive up to Amish country sometimes, to Miller's Dry Goods in Charm, to get our solid colors. The owner wasn't allowed to sell prints, because she was Amish. And then the prints that were available . . . were always little bitsy prints, so you could never get anything bold without going to a drapery shop. People today don't have any clue about any of that.

—Nancy Crow, interview, 2004

Nancy Crow

Loudonville, Ohio, Nancy Crow's hometown, lies near the heart of the state, a rural area nestled in the gently rolling hills near Mohican State Park where her family has lived since pioneer times. Born August 31, 1943, Nancy was the youngest of eight children. Her upbringing and the death of her father when she was twelve profoundly altered her world. Her father held high standards and was often strict, but at the same time was entirely devoted to his family and encouraged his children to be creative. Nancy said, "I will tell you that, because I was growing up in a family of artists, that I had always an incredibly strong drive. I knew I had to be successful. 'Successful' doesn't have anything to do with money. . . . I had to be as good as I could be with what I was given to work with."[60] Her father, she says, "believed that women should have every chance. And so I think he was way before his time, when you consider that was in the 1940s, and insisted that every single one of his five daughters go to college. . . . In my family I always felt . . . there were no limitations."[61]

Art was always a part of her life. As a child, Nancy attended a preschool focused on creating art. She remembers loving "the processes of cut-paper work and gluing cut-outs onto another sheet of paper. It follows that I loved cutting shapes out of fabric and piecing those shapes together."[62] She was also inspired by an eccentric neighbor, Sadie Chesrown, who had studied at the Cleveland School of Art (now CIA) in the 1920s. Chesrown had a house full of art, art in progress, handwoven rag rugs, doors painted with outdoor scenes, and impromptu collages. Nancy loved to visit her home,

and continued to do so until Chesrown's death in 1986.

In 1961, Crow went off to college at Ohio State University in Columbus, switching to fine arts after two weeks in the home economics program. In the course of her studies, she traveled to Mexico City, studying art at the city college there. This was her first introduction to the Hispanic cultures whose influence appeared in her artwork later, when she had the opportunity to live in Ecuador and Brazil after her marriage to John Stitzlein in 1965.

Crow began her MFA studies at Ohio State in the mid-1960s, majoring in ceramics with a minor in weaving, and graduated in 1969. She remembers the encouragement she received from her ceramics professor, Edgar Littlefield, and her solid foundation in design. Crow cites two lasting impressions from graduate school. First, she describes her sense of searching for an appropriate medium: "Something inside me knew that [ceramics] really wasn't 'it,' and even as I started . . . getting more and more serious about weaving, that didn't sit right. I knew there was something wrong, and I didn't know what it was." Second, Nancy describes how the principle of symmetry was presented: "[In graduate school] symmetry is not good enough. . . . That was always hanging over my head as a quiltmaker, because . . . symmetry is such an important principle of quiltmaking." At a pivotal time in Crow's career, in the early 1990s, she would make a significant break from symmetry in her work (see page 100).

Crow made her first quilt, with her mother's help, during a two-year stint in Brazil, when she was pregnant with her first son. Returning to Cambridge, Ohio, she continued to weave: "At that time I considered myself a serious tapestry weaver and worked

hard at it, while also raising two very small boys . . . but one day I ended up down at the Senior Citizens' Center asking if I might join the quilters, to watch them work if nothing else."[63] She later invited the group to her home to quilt, and they began to meet weekly and share a potluck lunch. "Those quilting bees are some of my fondest memories." The Cambridge Senior Center is where Crow met Berenice Dunlap, who showed her an antique Bear's Paw quilt from her family. Nancy recalled, "The impact of that quilt changed my life. I could not get over the boldness . . . the immense simplicity of design . . . the use of black." The thought now occurred to her that quilts could be art.

In 1974, the young family moved to Athens, Ohio, where Nancy opened a basket shop, which she had for two years. In Athens, she discovered the well-respected, but short-lived, textile department at Ohio University, and joined the community's very active textile guild. Like many of her contemporaries around the state, it was through this group that she became engaged with like-minded artists. Although Crow and her group of friends were all weavers, they began to experiment with making quilts as an art form. Nancy recalls, "I couldn't even begin to understand why we started making quilts. We all wanted to do it." She remembers "the excitement at knowing we were on the edge, the verge of 'something' not yet articulated."[64]

Nancy Crow with her first quilt, *Red and Black Crosses*, *1970–71*. Nancy Crow and Rachel Kensett Crow. 64" x 78". Hand-pieced and appliquéd cotton. This photograph of the only quilt she and her mother worked on together was taken at Nancy's home in Athens in 1976. Nancy says, "My mother . . . came down to help out with the new baby, but instead I talked her into working on my quilt. It was she who did most of the appliqué and the piecing." Photo courtesy of the artist.

Tramp Art, 1983. Nancy Crow. 54" x 65". Pieced cotton, hand-quilted by Rose Augenstein. Though her final break from symmetry came later, this piece, inspired by Nancy's collection of Tramp Art, is one of her earliest explorations combining her trademark piecing techniques in an asymmetrical composition. Photo by John Seyfried.

By 1976, Crow began to lose her enthusiasm for weaving, focusing instead on her quilts. Within three years, she had packed up her looms for good. "My great love has always been color and I wanted to use it in a large format. The slow process of tapestry weaving . . . was increasingly frustrating. I could see only a small portion of what I was doing. . . . I did not realize at that time that piecing [quilt] tops could or would be just as time consuming."[65]

By the mid-seventies, Crow was already showing her work around the state. By 1977–78, "word was traveling fast, slides were passed around, traded, and finally we became aware of this enormous enthusiasm radiating out from a small number of hardworking women and men who were dedicated to producing serious work."[66] Ideas and practical solutions to working limitations were freely

Quilting bee at Nancy Crow's Athens home, January 1976. Nancy Crow (*center*) and her friends learned precious skills during their get-togethers. Here, they quilt Nancy's *Whirligig* on a frame set up in the living room. Photo courtesy of Nancy Crow.

exchanged in the charged atmosphere. The practice of working on celotex boards on the wall, a solution her husband John had come up with to quiet Nancy's complaints about spreading her work all over the floor, began to catch on throughout the quilting community.

What Penny McMorris called "the first quilt symposium" was held in Ithaca, New York, in 1976. Nancy Crow recognized the importance of such conferences, not just as networking opportunities, but for the evolution of the movement: "I'm not so sure quilting would have developed as it did if it hadn't been for the teaching system offered by the quilting conferences."[67] Classes in quilting continued to spread like wildfire, giving those artists who taught, like Crow, an income aside from the sale of their artwork. The scope of Nancy Crow's influence through her teaching around the world is inestimable. In Ohio, nearly every artist I interviewed has felt the influence of Nancy's giving nature, and many took their first quiltmaking classes from her.

In 1979, Nancy Crow said good-bye to her dear friends in Athens and moved to the family's farm in Baltimore, Ohio. She found the transition difficult. "For the first time," she later wrote, "I began to suffer a 'profound depression.' I could not work, I had no interest in quilts anymore. I cried most of the time. . . . Whenever I walked outside I felt a 'renewal.' So I took that as my clue, picked up my camera and began walking the farm, every part of it, day after day, looking, training my eye until I finally began 'seeing.'"[68] She soon began construction on the first of several studios, paid for with money she had earned from her teaching and artwork sales. By the mid-eighties, Nancy had found her groove of working in a series, using the strip-piecing techniques of which she was already considered a master. Derived from techniques practiced by the Seminole Indians, strip-piecing had a powerful hold on Crow. Each new refinement," she says, "led to new understanding. I soon realized it would take a lifetime to learn to use it effectively and sensitively."[69]

While Nancy Crow still lived in Athens, she and her friends had sought to achieve increased visibility for the new work being done in quilts, by now all over the country. Approached by a friend from the textile guild, Harriet Anderson, to teach a workshop, Crow told her that the real need was a place to exhibit. Everything soon fell into place in Athens, Ohio, where, in 1979, a small group of women was about to change the landscape of the art world.

The Big Bang and the New Universe

THROUGHOUT THE 1970S AND 1980S, THE unprecedented popularity of quilts was evidenced by the proliferation of quilt shows, books, magazines, and workshops. In Ohio, quilt guilds focused on traditional quiltmaking were formed in virtually every county. When a guild became too large, another would form, and many quilters belonged to several local guilds and small groups, as well as national organizations such as the National Quilter's Association (NQA, formed in 1969) and the American Quilter's Society (AQS, formed in 1985). In northeastern Ohio alone, there were so many guilds that, in 1987, the Northeast Ohio Regional Quilters Council (NEORQC) was established to coordinate efforts between the guilds, shops, and teachers. By 1997 this organization represented 66 of the 100 or more guilds in the region, 35 quilt shops, and 35 teachers.

While traditional in nature, the guilds nurtured hobbyists and offered a meeting ground for the exchange and quick spread of ideas and techniques. Often hosting speakers and workshops, the state's guild network also offered opportunities for quilt artists to supplement their incomes and gain a following through teaching.

Despite the snowballing effect of the quiltmaking revival, artists who were making quilts were frustrated with the few exhibition venues available to them.[1] Ohio's numerous universities and regional art centers were showing their work on occasion, but such exhibits were sporadic. The only consistent forum to show quilts remained historical societies, state or county fairs, or quilt guild shows. Meanwhile, in the guilds, tensions were arising between traditionalists, hobbyists, and the makers of art quilts. In a 1988 interview, Cincinnati artist Elaine Plogman said, "I wonder when some of the large

Classified ad, 1982. By the early 1980s, there were so many quilters in the state that an entrepreneur first ran this classified ad for listings in the new *Ohio Quilt Directory* in the May 1982 issue of *Quilter's Newsletter Magazine*, the most popular quilting magazine of the time.

and 'important' quilt shows are going to stop bestowing awards principally on the basis of how finely a piece is quilted and a corner mitered. . . . We are turning ourselves into quilting machines when we place more . . . value upon the quality of the work than on the design of the work."[2] In an interview for *Ohio Pioneers of the Art Quilt,* Nancy Crow recalled, "Penny McMorris gave us that chance up at Bowling Green [in 1976] . . . then Ohio University gave us a chance to show our quilts . . . during the '70s. . . . Everything was for traditional quilts. It was very hard to find venues."[3]

In every field of art, the work of an artist is supported by cultural institutions, collectors, curators, critics, and organizers. The first important art quilt collections, the James collection and the Walsh collection (assembled by Penny McMorris),[4] lent further legitimacy to the field. Several Ohio artists and organizers worked actively to support the growth of the art quilt and became participants in the worldwide explosion of the medium. Ohio filmmakers, like Luanne Bole-Becker, and supportive curators and gallery directors, such as Daniel Butts III in Mansfield, Penny McMorris in Bowling Green, Ricky Clark in Oberlin, Hilary Fletcher in Athens, and Renee Steidle, juror in the first Quilt National and owner of Gallery 200 in Columbus, would expand the audience for art quilts and, in some cases, profoundly affect the careers of Ohio's quilt artists in years to come.

Penny McMorris

In an interview, Penny McMorris emphasized Ohio's prominent role in redefining the quilt: "One of the exciting things about being in Ohio is that we are in the center of the country and the quilt action. There is so much going on on the East and West coasts, but where quilts are concerned, we are very much it."[5] The fledgling art quilt movement came to fruition in Ohio and, eventually, across the nation in large part because of the curiosity and energy of women like Penny McMorris of Bowling Green, Ohio.

Born in 1943 in Wisconsin, Penny, like many other women of her generation, went to college, married, and had children. "I was a young mother back in the late '60s whose life centered around housework and children. I felt isolated and a bit bored, and I ached to be involved in something beyond the walls of my home. Since I was at the tag end of a generation brought up to believe that mothers of young children didn't work unless they had to, the idea of going out and getting a job never even occurred to me."[6] Still, she says, "I was frantic to have some other focus, and I wanted to make some money to legitimize whatever I did . . . and for some reason, I really wanted to rise to the top of it. Ambition was very important to me then."[7]

In the late 1960s, the young family moved to Bowling Green for a few years, and then to North Carolina, where McMorris took advantage of easy access to the fabric mills in the region and began a small business creating patchwork garments. She recalled, "It was lovely that at that time no one else was doing this, so it was a very hip thing to be doing."

Moving back to Ohio in the early 1970s, she retained that advantage: "When we came back to Bowling Green, I was . . . the only quilter that anyone knew, so being the first . . . got me a lot of attention. It was very easy to get that kind of attention at that time and easy for me have this little home business."[8] She began to teach quilting classes at the Bowling Green adult education program and in community colleges, traveling as necessary. "Gradually patchwork led me out of the house and into the world. I began making pillows and quilts to sell, which led to teaching quilting, which in turn led to organizing a juried show. And it was this show [Ohio Patchwork '76] which proved to be the turning point in my involvement with quilts."[9] McMorris realized then that she was witnessing the beginning of a new quilt movement.

Having enjoyed her growing contact with quilters during her years of teaching, McMorris realized she could reach a larger audience through television. She approached her local PBS station with a program idea, but nothing happened. Even though she maintained contact with the new quilters she had discovered, McMorris enrolled in the art history master's program at BGSU and "kind of dropped out of the interest in quiltmaking." After completing her master's degree in 1978, she went to work as curator of the Owens Corning art collection.

In 1980, Penny McMorris got a call from the local PBS station, asking her to do the series she had originally proposed. "I wasn't doing anything in quilts from '78 to '80. My first instinct was to say, 'No' . . . but . . . something stopped me and I said, 'Yes.'" *Quilting with Penny McMorris* was filmed in Bowling Green as well as on location, with episodes featuring a Quilt National exhibition, the Cleveland Institute of Art, and Miami University's Craft-Summer program in Oxford, Ohio. Most shows included artist interviews and showed the artwork of many of the artists she had met during the Ohio Patchwork '76 exhibit.

She enjoyed doing the shows, and modestly describes their success: "It was right place, right time. . . . They [WBGU-TV] could have continued it, had they had a personality who liked . . . being on

Penny McMorris, 1992. Instead of airing simple how-to programs, host McMorris of the PBS series *The Great American Quilt* (1991–92) engaged viewers with her own interests, presenting artist interviews, historical information, and trends, all the while keeping her finger on the pulse of the art quilt movement. *The Great American Quilt* promotional image courtesy WGBU-TV, Bowling Green, Ohio.

the promotional side of it, but my real interest was in the design and the people. I wasn't so interested in being a 'personality.' That wasn't me." After two series, she was ready to do something else.

The impact of McMorris's television series was enormous. *Quilter's Newsletter Magazine* reported that "1981 will be a banner year for American Quiltmakers. . . . In the last few years, museum and art gallery directors all over the country have been astonished by the popularity of quilt shows held in their exhibition halls. Now, with quality programming like the WBGU-TV series, the television medium will begin to recognize this late 20th century phenomenon."[10] Later that same year, *Quilter's Newsletter Magazine*'s editor reprinted a letter from WBGU-TV program manager Ron Gargasz: "Dear Mrs. Leman: We have been most successful in getting our 'Quilting' television series on PBS stations throughout the country. Your article . . . was, in large measure, responsible for our success. PBS program managers across the country have been inundated with letters and calls concerning our quilting series. Over 50 stations have already agreed to air the programs. . . . Thanks for your help!"[11]

As this letter implies, the series had a huge following, creating more and more viewers each time the programs were repeated. This first PBS series, and the ones that followed (*Quilting II with Penny McMorris* and *The Great American Quilt*), connected American quilters in a way that the periodicals of the time could not have done. Coinciding with the first Quilt National exhibits, *Quilting with Penny McMorris* ensured that Ohio art quilts were seen everywhere the programs were broadcast. Not only did Penny McMorris become a household name among quilters, but so did the guests she presented on her shows.

Quilt National: The Big Bang

In the background of this activity, in the late 1970s Ora and Harriet Anderson were trying to save an abandoned historic barn in rural Athens, Ohio. Their tireless efforts succeeded in 1978, when the barn was listed on the National Register of Historic Places and was organized as an art center. Nancy Crow still marvels at Harriet Anderson's dedication: "She wasn't a quiltmaker. Why did she care? If it hadn't been for Harriet and her husband, that barn never would have been saved."[12] Crow, Virginia Randles, and Françoise Barnes, along with an army of volunteers, are all to be credited for their extraordinary efforts in creating that first Quilt National exhibition. None of them had any way of knowing that Quilt National would quickly become the

Quilt National '79 flyer. Sent out along with Gary Schwindler's exhibition essay as promotional material, this was the only public documentation for the biennial exhibit until 1981, when the show's first catalog was published.

world's premiere showplace for art quilts. As exhibit director Hilary Fletcher describes it, the founders of Quilt National "picked up the gauntlet tossed into the fiber art community following the Whitney's enormous success."[13] Fletcher declared, "It was the Big Bang."[14]

Those who attended the first Quilt National in 1979 will remember the old cow barn's interior: "The trenches were still in the concrete floors; the stanchions were still in place; there was nothing covering the windows; and even though the cows had been gone for a decade, there were flies every-

Quilt National '99. Ora Anderson (who, with his wife, Harriet, was largely responsible for saving the Dairy Barn from destruction) and Nancy Crow at the Dairy Barn. Quilt National openings are always a great time for the artists to see old friends. Photo courtesy Hilary Fletcher.

where. While it is unimaginable that anyone would consider displaying quilts in such an environment today, the artists whose works were deemed 'not a quilt' (and therefore quite unacceptable to the organizers of the other quilt shows of the day) were delighted to finally have . . . a venue."[15]

As it still does today, the first Quilt National had three jurors, Massachusetts artist Michael James, Gallery 200 owner Renee Steidle, and Ohio University art history professor Gary Schwindler, who "first became aware of the visual power of quilts while teaching a course on Early American Art. It was then that he invited local quilters to address his classes."[16] There was a raffle quilt, made by Athens artist Françoise Barnes, and workshops and slide lectures by Beth and Jeffrey Gutcheon, Jean Ray Laury, and Wenda von Weise.

Ohio artists were strongly represented in the first exhibit: eleven out of the forty-five artists were Ohioans.[17] The handout that accompanied the exhibit (there was no catalog for the first show until later) contained a captivating and prophetic essay by Gary Schwindler, in which he made the point that "Quilt National '79 demonstrates eloquently two important phenomena characteristic of the contemporary American art scene. First, there is increasing prominence of the so-called 'crafts' within the broad spectrum of the plastic arts; and second, quilting in particular is emerging as a vital category of the fiber arts and possesses enormous expressive potential. American quilt making is now at a stage of experimentation and development as it prepares to take its place as a major form of artistic endeavor."[18]

It is impossible to discuss Quilt National without reference to Hilary (Morrow) Fletcher, in charge of the exhibition since 1982. Arriving in Athens in the early 1970s, Fletcher, a speech pathologist, was never much interested in quilts until she attended Quilt National '79 and the Jean Ray Laury lecture. Enthralled with what she saw and heard, Fletcher decided to volunteer at the Dairy Barn: "I was 'Miss Wednesday,'" she recalls. She attended the jury process for the 1981 exhibit and was put in charge of that year's quilt raffle. In fall 1982 she replaced Sara Gilfert, a fiber artist on the Ohio University art faculty, as director of the exhibit. Fletcher expertly shepherded Quilt National as the exhibition grew in scope and prestige

Quilt National '87. Old friends Susan Shie, Carolyn Robinson, and Petra Soesemann enjoy a moment. Shie's *Neighborhood with Comet Scar* hangs on the right behind the group, and was awarded Best of Show. Photo courtesy of Susan Shie.

to become an international, traveling show, with full-color catalogs chronicling the changes and the development of quilts as an art form. Penny McMorris, in acknowledging Fletcher's role as one of the leading authorities in the fiber art community, commented, "To me, Hilary Fletcher is Quilt National. . . . I'm a great fan of hers and don't think enough people realize how much credit she is due for making Quilt National the success it is."[19]

From a dilapidated dairy barn in Appalachian Ohio to its meteoric rise to the world's premiere venue for art quilts, the influence of Quilt National is incalculable. Like the Whitney show in the 1970s, Quilt National serves as the dividing line between what came before and what was to follow.

The show is not without its critics, some of whom find the definition of a quilt too limiting, excluding the best new work or unintentionally excluding young, emerging artists who do not identify themselves as quiltmakers. Some feel the show has outlived its usefulness, believing it helps maintain a "quilt ghetto" instead of introducing art quilts to the larger art world. But in the end, Quilt National succeeds in providing the highest visibility for the medium. Showing in the exhibit is the goal of any artist committed to making art quilts. As Linda Fowler points out, "Quilt National brings together people who are exploring . . . so you get a sampling of what is going on everywhere."[20]

Shock Waves from the Big Bang

And thus the exciting 1970s drew to a close, punctuated by the resounding success and worldwide impact of the Quilt National exhibition. By the early 1980s, the "Big Bang" began to create a new universe for art quilts and careers for the artists.

For example, in 1979, Ricky Clark, a leader of the Oberlin quilting community since the 1960s, went

The Artist as Quiltmaker IV, 1990. Juror Terrie Hancock Mangat and curator Ricky Clark go over notes in preparation for the object jury. Photo courtesy FAVA archives.

to see the first Quilt National exhibition. Many of the quilts, she recalled, were hung on the stanchions, "so you could see the front and the back. . . . I still remember these women were primarily artists rather than quiltmakers. . . . I remember one in particular, and on the back, there was a knot and . . . this long strand of thread hanging down. . . . Their technique was very poor."[21] Still, she encouraged her friend Evalena Briers to attend: "If you don't do anything else all summer, pick up your color camera and go down to Athens for Quilt National '79. It's a superb exhibit; 'quilt show' is a misleading term— it's really a contemporary art exhibit, with quilting as the medium. It's a major milestone in acknowledging quilts as art."[22]

Clark, an early member of the Fireland Association for the Visual Arts (FAVA), founded in Oberlin in 1979, served on the planning committee responsible for seeing what other regional art centers were doing.[23] Inspired by Quilt National, Clark founded the Artist as Quiltmaker (AQM) exhibition at FAVA. First held in 1984, AQM, like Quilt National, is a biennial exhibition. The two shows are held in alternating years, with the astounding result that art quilts have been exhibited in Ohio every year since 1983. Narrower in scope than Quilt National, the first two AQM exhibits were limited to entries from Ohio and contiguous states. Beginning with the 1988 exhibit, entries were accepted from the United States and Canada. At FAVA, gallery director Susan Edwards Harvith oversaw and carefully documented the exhibitions, curated by Clark. In 1989 Susan Jones took charge and raised the visibility of the exhibition. Jones, like Fletcher, always had to work to change many viewers' preconceived ideas about the quilts in the exhibition, through lectures, gallery talks, and wall signs.[24]

The Artist as Quiltmaker VI, exhibition poster, 1994. Without benefit of a catalog, this poster is the next best thing, illustrating the work of eleven of the pieces in the show, selected by juror Penny McMorris, including *Birds in the House* by Columbus artist Suzanne Evenson and *Blazing Skeletons* by Lakewood artist Nina Vivian Huryn. Poster designed by Sue Jones. Image courtesy FAVA archives. Photo by John Seyfried.

Both the rescued Dairy Barn and FAVA are among Ohio's oldest regional art centers, hosting numerous prestigious exhibitions, although the art quilt exhibitions remain the most popular. Other regional and national art quilt exhibitions have developed over the years in nearly every state and many countries, but Ohio's are the longest-lived, providing an excellent source for researchers to study trends in the evolution of the medium. Clark feels there is a real advantage in a biennial exhibition, especially from a historian's perspective, in that subtle changes and trends are readily seen in each exhibit.

In Ohio, another important statewide exhibit was held when the Canton Art Institute was persuaded by Sharon D'Atri (now Carpenter) to present an exhibit focused solely on Ohio quilts. Opening in the winter of 1982, Ohio Quilts: A Living Tradition was curated by D'Atri and her friend Jane Reeves, an art history major. The exhibit was promoted as "a salute to many exceptionally talented quiltmakers for their achievements over the past one hundred and eighty years."[25] A color catalog with excellent text documented this exhibition of Ohio's antique, Amish, and contemporary art quilts. After a year of research preparing for the exhibition, Reeves, not yet active as an art quilter, was already actively promoting textile art in Canton, and says, "It totally changed my life."[26] She was seeing art quilts for the first time, and soon began to make them herself.

Ohio Quilts: A Living Tradition, exhibition poster, 1982. This poster accompanied the catalog of the exhibition, and illustrated art quilts made by Terrie Hancock Mangat and Nancy Crow. Image courtesy of the Canton Art Institute. Photo by John Seyfried.

Whatever else you think they were (different, weird, terrible, wonderful), the seventies were certainly exciting. . . . The eighties should be even more exciting because contemporary quilters have really just begun to scratch the surface of their ingenuity and creativity in quilt design. I feel that during this decade they will enrich the traditions of quiltmaking and bring to the art new directions which will make this period one of the most important in the history of American quilts.

—Bonnie Leman (editor), *Quilter's Newsletter Magazine*, January 1980, 2

The Second Wave

Art Quilt Pioneers of the 1980s

THE QUILTMAKING REVIVAL CONTINUED TO grow exponentially throughout the 1980s. The field of quilt research also expanded, as quilt historians such as Ohio's Ricky Clark and Virginia Gunn played a leading role in the ongoing development of the American Quilt Study Group (AQSG), which in 1980 began its yearly publication of major quilt research papers in *Uncoverings*. The invention of the rotary cutter revolutioned quiltmaking as many quiltmakers sought ways to accelerate the process. Machine quilting developed into an art form of its own, as manufacturers created new machine feet and threads to meet the demand. Households acquired personal computers, enabling artists to design more quickly using programs such as McMorris and Neumann's Electric Quilt.[1] The Internet, which would blossom in the coming decade and connect quiltmakers in unheard-of ways, was in its infancy. In this atmosphere, an increasing number of Ohio quilt artists emerged, many gaining immediate recognition, due in no small part to the visibility of Quilt National. This second wave of quilt artists, some of whom equaled

or surpassed the achievements of the pathbreakers, benefited from the dedication and success of the art quilt pioneers as the movement roared through the decade and into the next.

The pioneers continued to break new ground in the 1980s and developed large bodies of mature work. Some, such as Nancy Crow and Wenda von Weise, applied for and received the recognition of Ohio Arts Council and National Endowment for the Arts grants, the first of many to be awarded to Ohio's quilt artists. Instead of the isolation that had characterized the beginnings of the art quilt movement, the artists of the second wave discovered a supportive community. In time, they in turn served as mentors for the artists who would follow. Like their predecessors, with few exceptions, the artists of the second wave grew up with sewing skills, and several had a history of quiltmaking in their families. Many took a few workshops early in their careers from the pioneer artists, who were by this time already well known. In 1983, Nancy Crow wrote, "Since no college or university offers a degree in this art, most quiltmakers learn from others through what must be one of the most organized networks of artists ever to exist."[2] Through such classes, exhibitions, a few university textile programs and continuing education programs, even guilds and fabric stores, they began to see each others' work and get to know each other. Still others left behind traditional art degrees in painting, sculpture, and printmaking and turned to fabric instead.

The artists of the second wave were also pioneers, bringing new and fresh voices to the movement, and a new sophistication built on the foundation of professionalism created in the previous decade. As the two groups mingled during the heady days of the 1980s, the bar was set higher, and making a mark in the growing field became more difficult. Those whose work had not evolved beyond the aesthetics acceptable in the 1970s dropped out of the sphere of influence at the same time that the new artists were gaining recognition. As early as 1983, Nancy Crow wrote, "When I began to exhibit work in the late 1970s, it was easier to make a splash because everything was still relatively new and not that many artists had turned to this form. Today, the work must be far more original."[3]

Clare Murray and Jane Reeves became acquainted during the 1982 Ohio Quilts exhibit held at the Canton Art Institute, on which Reeves had worked. Nancy Crow already knew Reeves and, upon later meeting Murray in a workshop she was teaching, Crow suggested that Murray contact Reeves when she returned to Canton. The two met and became the soul of the art quilt movement in Canton. Like other Ohio artists, they benefited from their networking with Nancy Crow. In 1984, both were invited to participate in Emerging Quiltmakers at the Columbus Cultural Arts Center, one

of the earliest exhibitions Crow organized to help promote the work of new artists.[4] Murray vividly recalls the exhibit: "That was the most astounding quilt show. . . . I came home from that, and I was just on such a high, not so much because I was in it, but because the things I saw were so exciting and amazing to me. I was totally blown away when I saw . . . what people were doing."[5] That same month, Reeves and Murray exhibited together at The Little Art Gallery in Canton, the first of several contemporary quilt exhibits there.

Clare Murray

Clare Murray was born in Canton in 1950. Her mother and grandmother sewed and quilted, but Clare's desire to learn to sew dawned in high school, when her mother, in a single evening, made her a new outfit to wear on "Civies Day" instead of her usual Catholic school uniform.

After graduation from Kent State University (KSU) and five years as a first-grade teacher, Murray left the classroom in 1976 to open a fabric store, the Cloth Tree, where she offered classes in sewing, crafts, and, eventually, quiltmaking. In 1979 she signed up for a three-week quilt design class

Symphony, 1981. Clare Murray. 90" x 90". Machine-pieced cotton, blends, velvet, satin, and sheers, hand-quilted. Using strip-piecing techniques and color gradations, as well as the reflective properties of shiny and matte fabrics, Murray's asymmetrical composition is a good example of her early pieced work, which often had an architectural theme. According to the Ohio Quilts catalog, in this work she hoped "to show the way a piece of music grows" and integrated piano keys and musical notes into the design. Photo by John Seyfried.

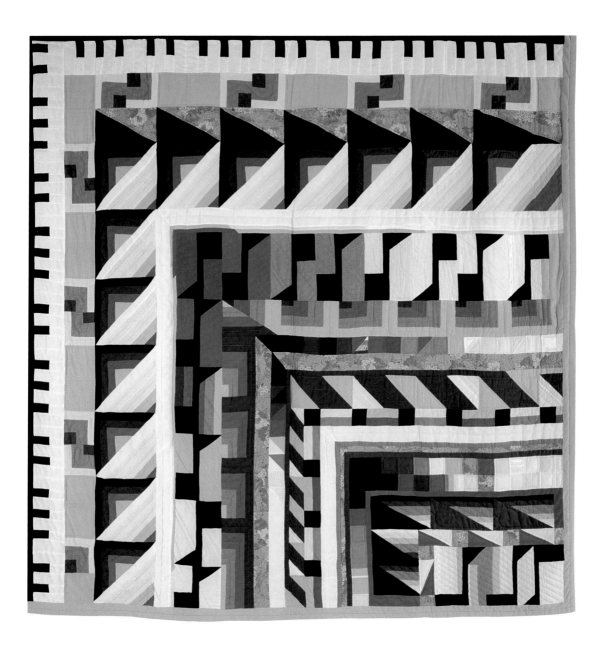

at Haystack School taught by Beth and Jeffrey Gutcheon. Through the Gutcheons, she heard about Quilt National '81, and went to Athens to see it. Inspired, she sold her shop and converted the first floor of her home into studio space. When she took the workshop with Nancy Crow, she brought her quilt *Symphony* with her. Crow praised the design, Murray recalled, but told her, "These are really cheesy fabrics."

A dyeing workshop at Haystack in the early 1980s enhanced Murray's surface design techniques. She began selling hand-dyed fabrics through a small mail-order business, and taught her artist friends the techniques. This was the birth of the Dye Group, which continues to meet on a regular basis, a source of great support and idea exchange in northeastern Ohio.[6]

In 1990, Murray returned to Kent State to pursue a BFA degree. She recalls a turning point that occurred in a sculpture class: "The teacher knew that I came from a fibers background, so he said, 'Always try to bring something from your sewing . . . into whatever else it is you're doing, and try to take something from this new stuff and put it in.' . . . I pass that along to my students today."[7] Murray went on to earn an MFA in 2001.

Like some of the pioneers and many other quilt artists working today, Murray's mastery of surface design techniques and exploration of materials and content have proven fruitful as she continues to risk following the path of her ideas. Much of her work today is representative of a trend toward art that challenges the line between quiltmaking and mixed media constructions, much of which no longer fits what has become the accepted and sometimes limiting definition of an art quilt. Murray says, "I make work for myself. I make what I want and then I try to find venues to exhibit it in. . . . I never was one to read contest rules and try to make something for [the competition]." It remains to be seen how this trend will be integrated into the field. It poses a problem for the future of the medium, because many young emerging artists are creating this type of crossover work and do not necessarily identify themselves with the art quilt field. This issue was addressed by curator Robert Shaw in an article for *Fiberarts:* "[Jack Walsh and Penny McMorris] have found that some of the freshest quilt work being done today is by artists who choose not to participate in the many contests, shows, and workshops of 'art quilts' that have proliferated in the past decade or so."[8]

Interior #3, 1993. Clare Murray. 45" x 60". Appliquéd, collaged, dyed, painted, and embellished cotton and sheers, machine- and hand-quilted. Work from Murray's BFA exhibition at Kent State University consisted of a series of quilts and paintings based on the architecture of chairs, windows, and doors. Photo courtesy of the artist.

Jane Reeves

Jane (Witter) Reeves was born in 1937 in Canton, where her family has lived for generations. Her family had quilts when she was growing up and, like most young girls of the time, she learned to sew and make her own clothes. After college, she married and spent much of the 1960s, her "domestic decade," learning to cook and volunteering at various art institutions. Looking back, Reeves thinks that "the whole cultural change of the '60s and '70s . . . promoted the craft movement" and was a validation of handwork. "It was at a time of just enormous upheaval and change, and just about every assumption you grew up with was shaken. . . . It was an interesting period."[9]

When Reeves decided to begin making quilts in 1981, she wanted to build on traditional handwork by creating her own designs. She purchased Michael James's books and completed all the design exercises. She then took two workshops, one with Nancy Crow at her barn studio and one with Michael

James, held during Quilt National. Jane Reeves, Clare Murray, and another Canton friend, Karen Pollard, had signed up for the class, but at the last minute, Murray could not go. Reeves said, "That's when I met Lois [Carroll].[10] . . . She came down to . . . Canton [from Parma]. I drove her and Karen to Athens, and we spent the week there." "Nancy [Crow] was a very dynamic influence on a lot of people in that period, and really promoted contemporary quilts, . . . [but] the biggest influence on me in the beginning was Michael James. The things that he made . . . twenty-five years ago . . . these gorgeous colors, so much movement . . . just blew me away."

For a decade beginning in the mid-eighties, Reeves, like many of the other artists, spent a lot of time doing commissions, especially for corporations. "At one time it was very trendy for companies to have big art collections," she observes. "All of a sudden, that just . . . dried up." Now living in North Carolina, Reeves maintains a private studio and an exhibition space in a converted Woolworth's store in Asheville. Her work has evolved away from hardline geometrics to softer, narrative quilts. Influenced by the media experimentation she was exposed to in the Dye Group, she began working in paper in the mid-1990s and assemblages late in the decade. She says, "I'm not very analytical about my work. . . . I kind of have [my grandchildren] in the back of my mind. . . . They'll be able to look at these [artworks] long after I'm gone . . . and learn something about their family from them."

Postmodern XIII, 1987. Jane Reeves. 72" x 80". Hand-dyed and machine-pieced cotton, hand-quilted. Part of Reeves's *Postmodern* series, this piece, which was shown in Quilt National '89, is representative of much of the artist's early work. Using geometric abstractions focused on color, shape, and the illusions of space and movement, the work evokes abstract architectural themes consistent with Reeves's interests. She graduated from college in 1959 with a degree in art history with a special interest in classical architecture. In Canton, she was active in the historical preservation movement that began in the 1970s, and also worked in textile preservation for the McKinley Museum.

During the 1980s, Columbus, Ohio, was destined to become another worldwide hub for the art quilt movement. Before there was an active quilting community in the metropolitan state capital, the Liturgical Art Guild and the Weaver's Guild attracted artists interested in fiber. By 1980, quiltmaking was catching fire, and artists such as Suzanne Evenson, Judith Vierow, and Carole Serio began their careers. In 1979 and 1980, Serio ran three classified advertisements for her Quilting Teacher Seminar in *Quilter's Newsletter Magazine* and held an exhibition of her students' work in Columbus's main public library. Byzantium, one of the state's earliest and best-supplied bead stores, opened in Columbus in 1985, providing a source for embellishment materials as well as unusual fabrics and niche periodicals. Artists from all over the state made regular treks there to pick up supplies not available elsewhere. In retrospect, however, the serendipitous meeting of Nancy Crow and Linda Fowler deserves credit for putting the city on the radar of the worldwide art quilt community.

"Net"—Egyptian AllMother, 1989. Judith Vierow. 56" x 92". Appliquéd, printed and batiked cotton, buttons, hand- and machine-quilted. Many of the artist's quilts during her decade in the field explored feminine and goddess themes. Net, in ancient Egypt, was the source of all creation. This quilt was exhibited in Quilt National '91. Photo by D. R. Goff.

Borghese, 1996. Jane Reeves. 43" x 55". Hand-dyed cotton embellished with paint and ink, machine-pieced and appliquéd, hand-quilted. To evoke the peeling and crumbling surface of an old stucco wall, the artist partially obscured written quotations and drawings of architectural fragments with layers of paint. The quilting design outlines a street map of Rome. Photo courtesy of the artist.

Hopescape XIII (detail), 1997. Linda Fowler. In her more recent works, Fowler has developed increasing depth in her compositions, enhanced by the use of paint, hand-dyed fabrics, and other surface design techniques. Photo by John Seyfried.

Linda Fowler

Linda Fowler, born in Los Angeles in 1944, moved with her family to Columbus in the early 1950s. Her parents encouraged her early interest in art by keeping her supplied with art materials. She also learned to sew and do needlework, which became an integral part of her life. As she grew into adulthood, she felt called to the church. She joined the Sisters of St. Joseph order in 1961, completed her education, and began teaching. Early on she became involved in the influential Liturgical Art Guild in Columbus, where she met fellow artist Deborah Melton Anderson. Both women have spent many years creating commissioned church vestments, altar cloths, and banners for congregations around the region.

While pursuing graduate studies at the University of Dayton in the late 1960s, Fowler enrolled in a weaving class. Encouraged by her friend, painter Dick Barry, to pursue her artistic interests, she received permission from her order to study art. In 1976 she returned to Ohio State University (OSU), and completed her BFA and MFA degrees in the fiber department. Although she was a weaving major, she took advantage of OSU's strong photography department to learn how to develop film and create silk screens on paper. In 1980, with another Columbus artist, Judith Vierow,[11] she attended the Craftsummer program at Miami University, where they studied batik and silk-screening on fabric. Her first quilts were made using these techniques; she read Michael James's books to learn how to assemble the fabrics into a quilt.[12]

Venece, 1983. Linda Fowler. 52" x 52". Pieced and appliquéd cotton, hand-quilted. Fowler's early work contains all the elements that have become synonymous with her style: an arched shape containing a path leading to a doorway, metaphorical representations of her deep spiritual life, and her interest in architecture. As her work evolved, the compositions became less symmetrical. Father Larry Nolan, the chaplain at her convent, devised the shaped hanging rods for her work. Linda says the difficulty of shipping the large rods caused her to focus on showing her work in galleries within driving distance. Photo by Kevin Fitzsimons.

In the late 1970s, Linda Fowler met Nancy Crow, whom she had invited to jury a Weaver's Guild exhibition in Columbus. In 1980, Fowler and Deb Anderson took a weeklong workshop with Crow, and turned to quiltmaking full-time. Fowler says that Crow "challenged her to question issues and focus on direction" and to begin thinking of working in a series.[13] For Fowler it was an easy transition from weaving to quiltmaking. Using a Navajo

Ameriflora I, 1992. Linda Fowler. 99" x 91". Cotton blends, paint, and paintsticks; machine-pieced, appliquéd, and quilted. One of a series of Fowler's architectural designs, this was made to celebrate a horticultural exhibition held in Columbus to recognize the 500th anniversary of the voyage of Christopher Columbus. Photo by John Seyfried.

tapestry loom, she had already been creating large shaped woven pieces that explored themes similar to the ones she would explore in her large shaped quilts. This work had been inspired by a trip to Greece, funded by a Ford Foundation grant, to study Greek weaving traditions, Fowler explained, "but then, I was taking pictures of the architecture, and that's what really influenced me."[14]

Fowler left the convent in 1988 and later married. She credits her years in the order for her ability to keep focus, slow down, and appreciate her natural environment. She continues her liturgical work, and finds that her artwork has evolved, representing what she feels is a greater connection between landscape and architecture. While much of her work can be found in churches, libraries, chapels, and health centers, she knows that many people cannot afford such large work. Like many of today's art quilters, Fowler has begun to create smaller, more intimate quilts, which are more affordable and scaled to the home environment.

The Art Quilt Network

In the early 1980s, Nancy Crow had invited Linda Fowler and Deborah Anderson to be part of a small and supportive group of artists from the area who would periodically get together to discuss their work. In 1987, Fowler and Crow decided to expand the experience by inviting a group of quilt artists to a retreat. Recalling the inspiration for this first get-together, Crow told New Hampshire artist Tafi Brown, "I had no one to talk to. Linda [Fowler] and I wanted to talk. The primary purpose of these meetings was intellectual stimulation for us and our work. There was a need to share ideas after long periods of solitude with our work."[15] Eight of the twelve artists invited, several from outside Ohio, attended this first retreat, called "Dialogue for Serious Quilters." It was held at the convent of Linda Fowler's order, Villa Madonna, and included a visit to Nancy Crow's studio in Baltimore, Ohio. The proceedings were tape recorded and documented by the volunteer historian, Tafi Brown, and included Nancy Crow reading letters sent by those unable to attend.[16] Brown recalled that she was "just about to explode with the desire to share thoughts, ideas, observations, to question others about their experiences, to meet others who were struggling with the loneliness, the self doubt, the income insecurities. . . . It was easy and pleasant to fall into very personal conversations in this convent, off by itself in the country."[17]

Building on the success of the first retreat, a second was held at Villa Madonna in November 1987, "Retreat for Serious Contemporary Quiltmakers." This time, twenty-six artists from around the United States and Canada participated.[18] These

Studio of Nancy Crow, Baltimore, Ohio, 1987. Retreat attendees Linda Fowler, Susan Kristoferson, Esther Parkhurst, and Nancy Crow go over discussion topics. Photo courtesy of Tafi Brown.

two 1987 retreats were the beginning of the Art Quilt Network (AQN), the oldest such group in the world. Limited to sixty active members, the group meets twice a year in Columbus for a three-day retreat.

In 1989, Nancy Crow created a second group, Art Quilt Network/New York (AQN/NY), for the convenience of those who found it difficult or impossible to travel to Ohio twice a year. Some artists, such as Deborah Anderson, retain membership in both groups. In either case, the retreats are intimate and informative, often including gallery visits, mini-workshops, slide shows, tips on professional development, and sometimes the planning of group exhibits. Deb Anderson observed, "One of the interesting things that happened with the Art Quilt Network is that, I would have thought that a lot of us might turn out to be Nancy Crow clones, or that we would all sort of make similar things. . . . It

doesn't work that way at all. That association is like giving each other permission to just do it whichever way we want to do it."[19]

Over the years, the Art Quilt Network has increased the visibility of art quilts in Ohio, but also has profoundly influenced the art quilt community. Because the membership size is limited and the waiting list is always full, artists around the country began to duplicate the organization. In the late 1980s and the 1990s many such groups formed as the field continued to grow: FACET in Chicago, Studio Art Quilt Associates (SAQA), the Art Quilt Alliance (AQA), the Contemporary QuiltArt Association (CQA), The Miami Valley Art Quilt Network (sponsors of a yearly exhibition in Dayton, Ohio), Quilt San Diego, and on the Web, ArtQuilts.net and Quiltart, "the Internet's largest mailing list for contemporary art quilters."

Studio of Linda Fowler, Villa Madonna, Columbus, Ohio, 1987. An unused reading room at the convent was converted into an art studio for Linda's use. Note the works in progress hanging on celotex boards leaning against the wall. Photo courtesy Tafi Brown.

The Quilt Surface Design Symposium

As the community of art quilters continued to grow, Nancy Crow and Linda Fowler seized on an idea designed to fill the still-existing void in professional fiber art education. From their experience in AQN, Fowler says, "we knew what it was like to have people come and stay for a while."[20] After seeking help from Marty Bowne, a friend experienced in organizing conferences, they held the first Quilt Surface Design Symposium (QSDS) in 1990 at the Pontifical College Josephinum in Columbus, the venue for the ongoing Art Quilt Network retreats.

Participants could choose from a wide array of intensive five-day workshops or sign up for independent study supervised by Nancy Crow. For those who were interested in attending without signing up for any classes, studio space was available to rent for the week. There was a vendor's mall as well as daily panel discussions moderated by faculty member and Cincinnati artist David Walker. In an article about the first symposium, written for the *Professional Quilter,* the experience of attending was still fresh in my mind: "In the classrooms there was intense work and growth coupled with joy in the art and renewed commitment to it. Students and faculty alike were free at any time to explore the work being done in other classrooms. No one was guarding techniques. On the contrary, both students and faculty were freely sharing ideas, techniques and fabric."[21]

In 2000 Nancy Crow stepped down from active participation in organizing the symposium, and Tracy Rieger stepped in to continue operations with Linda Fowler. In the past few years they have created the Quilt Surface Design Foundation, which funds symposium attendance for about ten students a year and hopes to provide an opportunity for young, emerging artists to attend. The recent addition of a juried student exhibition is another contribution to the community Fowler feels strongly about. By creating a venue for emerging artists and getting grants to film the shows and cover the expense of traveling the exhibits to other locations, the juried student exhibition encourages new artists to garner wider recognition of their work in what is now a very competitive field.

Now in its sixteenth year, the symposium has developed into a community of its own, where first-time attendees make important connections and find support, encouragement, and a new confidence, and returnees relish the one or two weeks they have to work, reconnect with old friends, and focus on their development away from their daily routine. Furthermore, the existence of the symposium has had a profound effect on the continued development of the medium, especially in the surface design arena.

Unlike other conferences, QSDS was organized for the quilt artist. . . . The people were of a like mind. All were interested in pursuing quiltmaking as an art, not a hobby or a pastime.

—Lynn Lewis Young (editor), *Art/Quilt Magazine,* premiere issue, 1994

Deborah Melton Anderson

"I have always loved working with fabric. . . . [D]uring the war, my mother would make little dresses out of the feed-bag fabric, so she taught me very early how to use the sewing machine."[22] Deborah Melton Anderson was born in Columbia, Missouri, in 1937. After completing college at the University of Missouri in 1959, she went to Cambridge, Massachusetts, to complete her master's degree at the Harvard Graduate School of Education. After graduating, she found a job in Harvard Square while her husband-to-be completed law school. In a store right around the corner from work, Deborah discovered Marimekko fabrics, and she was smitten, utilizing them for the next three decades in her liturgical work and in her earliest quilts.

The couple married in Missouri, then moved to Columbus, Ohio. In the early 1960s, Deborah joined the Liturgical Art Guild, formed in Columbus in the late 1950s, and found there support for her textile work and friendship with like-minded artists such as Linda Fowler and Ann Joyce, both of

Basilica Armen-Odzun, 1989. Deborah Melton Anderson. 39.5" x 42". Cotton Marimekko fabrics and cottons, machine-appliquéd and machine-quilted. Deborah says, "Because we were collecting Oriental rugs, and some were made by Armenians . . . I ran across a book at the library on Armenia, and there were some pictures of basilicas." That image was the inspiration for this work. Much of Anderson's work can be described as textiles inspired by textiles. Photo by John Seyfried.

whom later also turned to quiltmaking. Anderson has exhibited her work through the guild for the past forty years. As her work creating liturgical pieces began to grow, she recalls beginning to think about the course of her career: "I always thought I was making art. I took art classes. . . . I always did drawing. . . . The idea of copying something, working a kit, was just not in my blood. I always had to change something. . . . The issue for me in the '60s was, am I a professional artist, or not? [W]hen I started doing commissions for other churches and temples, other than my own . . . [I thought,] that makes me a professional."

By the late 1970s Anderson, a serious collector of textiles from all over world, was well versed in the textile traditions of many cultures. At antique shows, she would see quilts or quilt blocks, even occasionally purchased them, but had not begun to make them herself. When Linda Fowler asked if she would like to accompany her to a Nancy Crow workshop, she eagerly agreed. "It was just so exciting. . . . I designed various other things . . . but to have [Nancy] say, 'You can just make up your own designs'—I ran with that!" Soon, she and Fowler were invited by Crow to join Elizabeth Cave, Ruth Palmer, and other quilt artists from the area to be part of a small group. When the Art Quilt Network was formed, they participated enthusiastically in that group, as well.

"Nancy Crow was an influence. Not so much her designing, but her just doing it. Just go in your studio and carry out your ideas . . . and consider it important. That was what influenced me a great deal." Similarly, Deb felt the same surge of inspiration from watching the dedication and focus Virginia Randles brought to her work: "She realized that she

Pivots: Jerome County, Idaho (detail), 1999. Deborah Melton
Anderson. 25" x 75". Altered and heat-transferred photographs on cotton, textile ink, colored pencil. Using aerial
photographs of the Idaho landscape, Anderson created a
three-part narrative composition. The triptych is an ancient
iconographic format, and lends a spiritual feeling to her mu-
table composition. In this work, Anderson first used textile
inks and colored pencils to draw on the surface. Hand-
coloring and quilting on a textile surface add dimension
and a sense of the presence of the artist's hand. Photo by
Kevin Fitzsimons.

loved designing and constructing . . . quilts, so she went ahead and did it. She was considerably older than Nancy, but I think Nancy's energy and that group probably helped her make some of these decisions to go ahead. . . . I think when you see other artists who take their craft or their medium seriously, and really work at it, I think that's an inspiration."

In the late 1980s, Anderson says, "I became intrigued by the expressive possibilities of using photo transfers—a technology which grew out of the tee shirt business. Using my own photographs, a color laser copier, and a heat press, I began making quilts based on the transmogrification of my photos."[22] She was exposed to the technique during the creation of a community project in Columbus, The Public Book. Like Wenda von Weise in the 1960s, Anderson found the possibilities of combining photography and quiltmaking seductive. Instead of making silk screens, Anderson experimented with the newly available transfer paper technology and the possibilities of image manipulation and creative printing methods using the high-tech laser machines newly available in the computer age. Truly a pioneer and a recognized authority on such techniques, she has been influential in approach, as well as in the dissemination of knowledge about image transfer techniques. Anderson does not work exclusively with transfer techniques, and her work is not solely motivated by the techniques at her disposal. Instead, she "consider[s] these different fabrics and techniques to be . . . in my repertoire, and when I get an idea . . . whatever pleases me, I go with that technique."

The Back Boathouse, 1992. Deborah Melton Anderson. 56" x 42". Photo transfers on cotton using photographs by the artist. Hand- and machine-quilted. Photo courtesy of the artist.

Carolyn Mazloomi

Carolyn Mazloomi moved from Los Angeles to the Cincinnati, Ohio, area in the mid-1980s with her husband and three sons. Although the scope of her contribution to the art quilt field is more focused on the African American community nationally, it is important to acknowledge her pioneering efforts in creating community by advancing the visibility and voices of artists of color.

She was born in Louisiana in 1948 and grew up during the height of the civil rights movement. In recalling her early college years in Alabama, she said, "It was a terrible time. . . . I can remember Dr. King coming on the campus at Tuskegee recruiting students to hand out flyers. . . . My roommate at the time at this historic black institution was a white girl from Texas. . . . We couldn't go to Birmingham . . . to shop. We couldn't be seen together. It was dangerous times for that kind of friendship."[23] Mazloomi was not only affected by the civil rights movement brought about by the country's long history of racism, she lived it, and was even suspended from one university for student activism. In the 1980s, motivated by the memories of these experiences, she became an organizer and an advocate for quilt artists of color around the world.

I Dream of Africa, 1996. Carolyn Mazloomi. 54" x 72". Appliquéd and quilted cotton. Most of Mazloomi's works, which she calls story quilts, are created in a narrative style. Her quilts draw their inspiration from her interest in African American issues and the empowerment of women. Photo by Charles E. Martin.

She finished college at the University of Southern California in Los Angeles, earning a doctorate in aerospace engineering in 1984. A quilt collector since the 1970s, Mazloomi now has more than four hundred quilts in her private collection. When she saw a special quilt at a Dallas trade market in the late 1970s, she was inspired: "It was during the time when the Appalachian cooperatives were selling quilts wholesale to the trade . . . and I saw a quilt from Kentucky." She was motivated by the discovery of the prized patchwork quilt to teach herself to make quilts in the early 1980s. Looking for support, she founded the African American Quilt Guild of Los Angeles. She also placed an ad in *Quilter's Newsletter Magazine* asking any African Americans reading the ad to write. Eight people answered the ad. She recalls, "I had to find other African American quilters. That's a very isolating fact for any quilter coming from any minority. I hear it every day from minority quilters when they join guilds. They're the only one, and they always quilt different, because they're quilting from their cultural reference point."

In 1985 Carolyn Mazloomi founded the Women of Color Quilter's Network (WCQN) to foster and preserve the art of quiltmaking among people of color. Membership has grown to more than 1,700, and the group has several highly acclaimed national museum exhibitions to its credit. Mazloomi's goals have been accomplished. "I feel my most important work is not as a quiltmaker, but as an organizer. [Artists in the WCQN] are becoming recognized in a field that is not populated by a lot of people from our culture. . . . I want people to know they placed a footprint on the canvas of America."

Untrained in art, Mazloomi has nevertheless had substantial success in showing and selling her narrative-style quilts. The influence of her ethnicity is often obvious in her work, as is a feminist glance at the status of women. Although her first love is intricate patchwork, she says, "Unfortunately, I have never been able to make a quilt top with such precision. . . . I turned to appliqué because it was easy to do." In addition to regular exhibits at the Malcolm Brown Gallery in Cleveland, her work has been acquired by many prestigious museums, such as the Renwick, and private collectors, such as Whoopi Goldberg and Nelson Mandela. In support of a WCQN exhibition, in 1998 she published the highly acclaimed *Spirits of the Cloth,* the first book ever written about contemporary African American quiltmakers.

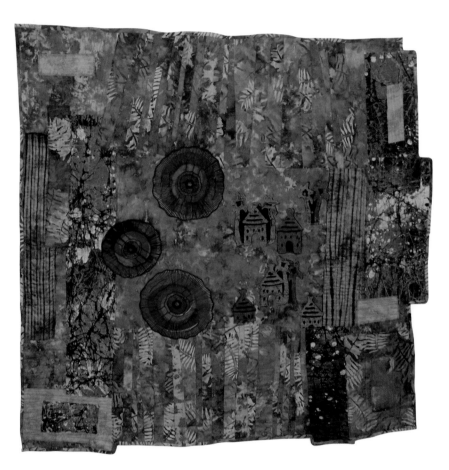

A New Journey, 2005. Carolyn Mazloomi. 65" x 74". Cotton, silk, appliqués, shells, beads, machine-quilted. Photo courtesy of the artist.

David Walker

Passion is a theme that runs throughout David Walker's life: passion for books, for inner knowledge, for teaching, for art, and an ongoing quest to discover how to keep passion alive during midlife. David, born in Chicago in 1942, and his older sister grew up in Mt. Clemens, Michigan, in what he describes as a "Tom Sawyer environment."[24] When he was in high school, his dad retired and moved the family to Pinellas Park, Florida, where David made the decision to be baptized in the Catholic Church.

After three years at the University of Florida, Walker left in 1963 and went to seminary in Rochester, New York. He had always wanted to teach, so when he saw a job posting while doing seminary work at Xavier College in Cincinnati, he interviewed and was hired. He completed a master's degree in education in 1979, and ended up teaching seventh grade for twenty-two years. Like Linda Fowler at the convent, Walker was quite isolated from the social and cultural revolution going on around him during his years in seminary in the 1960s. Instead, he learned to focus on self-discovery, a skill that has served him well throughout his life.

In the late 1970s, David was exploring many of the requisite handcrafts of the day, such as macramé and cross-stitch embroidery. In his yearly attendance at the local Appalachian Festival, he would always stop at Pat Nolan's weaving booth, and was pleased when a friend bought him a set of classes with her. He learned to make woven and braided rugs, which he also sold. In the late 1970s, Walker took Nolan's night class on making a quilted pillow

David Walker at the Quilt National '89 opening, Athens, standing before *Renascence for Rebecca* (61" x 55", commercial cottons and blends, control-bleached and dyed fabrics, beads, sequins and fabric paint; machine pieced and appliquéd). The title *Renascence* is taken from a poem by Edna St. Vincent Millay and celebrates the ability of the human spirit to renew itself. Photo courtesy Susan Shie.

top, and reports, "I sit on it now when I do my quilts." Pat loaned him a sewing machine, and he made an eight-pointed star quilt, and started a tradition of making crib quilts for expectant mothers at the school where he taught. He joined the large regional quilt guild, the Ohio Valley Quilters, and exhibited in an NQA show at Miami University in 1983, where he received an honorable mention award.

Already beginning to tire of making traditional patterns, David signed up for a quilting class with Jan Myers-Newbury at Miami University's Craft-Summer program in Oxford, Ohio. The next summer, he took a series of three week-long classes there with instructors Nancy Halpern, Michael James, and Nancy Crow. Thinking back, David

said, "That was the kicker. I was just amazed by what [Nancy] had to say more than what she did. . . . In those days . . . she walked into a classroom, and she held in her arms a pile of books, and we sat down at the beginning of the day, and she would talk about Van Gogh . . . [or] Frida Kahlo with great passion."

Walker has had a profound impact in the art quilt community through his artwork, articles, lectures, seminars, and workshops. In 1989, encouraged by Nancy Crow, he took a leap of faith and left his teaching post in the Catholic school system. At the same time, he decided to separate himself from the church, saying, "It just didn't make sense anymore, at all. [My] quilts . . . had a lot to do with the changes I was making in my spiritual life." Nancy had asked David to offer a workshop, his first, at the Quilt Surface Design Symposium in 1990. "In the first sentence of the workshop description I said something about 'discovering the spiritual resources' for our work. . . . It all started with that first class . . . and that's what my workshops have become known for."

Walker was a pioneer in his intuitive approach to teaching, giving his mostly midlife students new confidence. He began each class with a meditation time to help them get in touch with their work and their motivations. His instructions would follow:

Clare, 1983. David Walker. 54" x 52". Machine-pieced tessellated shapes, commercial and hand-dyed cotton, hand-quilted by Flora McMannis. Named for his cat Clare, this quilt was shown in the first Artist as Quiltmaker exhibit and is representative of Walker's early work. Although he had yet to add appliqué in this piece, his mature style is already apparent in the free and asymmetrical nature of the abstract composition. Photo courtesy the FAVA archives.

"You've got to start with right now. . . . You've got fabric, you've got thread, you've got a machine, you've got electricity. Let's put 'em all to work. Just sit with that for a while and come up with something. Let the passion emerge." He approaches his own personal narrative abstractions in the same manner, without advance planning, and he says the method has never failed him.

In the early 1980s, David Walker met Elaine Plogman, who was also a member of the Ohio Valley Quilter's Guild. Like many of his contemporaries, he eventually left the guild and joined alternative organizations, such as the newly formed Art Quilt Network. He and Plogman were also part of the Group of Six, an outgrowth of AQN. The group was formed locally so the artists could meet more frequently to provide mutual support. Jane Burch Cochran and Rebekka Seigel, both from nearby Kentucky; Gerry Fogarty, from Yellow Springs, Ohio; and Virginia Gaz, from Cincinnati, completed the group.

With an output of more than three hundred quilts to date, grants, and participation in a multitude of shows, including several Quilt National exhibits, Walker is one of the preeminent male quilt artists in the country. Although he has always felt a part of the group, being male in this predominantly female field has presented some unusual opportunities. "I've been invited to a lot of exhibitions . . . just for men, and I've refused all of them. I always say, 'I do not show my work in exclusive . . . shows.' I think that's divisive."

Virginia Randles was both friend and mentor to Walker, as she was to many. He remembers an example of her simple wisdom. "Virginia summed up an Art Quilt Network retreat discussion with this simple wisdom: 'What you think of yourself is the

most important thing in the world. No one else can do it for you.' Everyone immediately related to the truth of what [she] had said."[25]

Credo

I believe
that artists possess a particular vision
that can change and heal a society in distress.
I believe
that through hard work and relentless focus,
we can make a difference and bring
hope, light and understanding
to every dark and fearful place
within the human spirit.
I believe
that the world needs to know and experience
the unique vision and truth
that each artist possesses.
As an artist myself,
I believe that we are powerful beyond measure.[26]

Returning Home, 1994. David Walker. 48" x 41". Machine-embroidered appliquéd and quilted cotton, netting, control bleaching and overdyeing, stamping, beading. The third in a series of works, Walker says, "which began as a simple statement of how I had tired of grieving. I decided to throw all my unexpressed grief out into the universe, a fitting container in my mind, large enough for the stars and the planets and surely large enough to care for my grief as well." This piece was dedicated to friend Charlie Bolan, who died from complications as a result of AIDS. Permanent collection of the Ohio Craft Museum, Columbus, Ohio.

I didn't go to art school with the thought of preparing myself for a career. I went because this is important to me as a human being, and I'm going to school to get an education . . . to be a human being, not to get a job. . . . I think [students today] are desperately looking for [this] integrity.

—Petra Soesemann, interview, 2004

As in Ohio's other metropolitan areas, the group of second wave artists in the greater Cleveland area is a large and diverse one, tied together by local resources such as the Textile Art Alliance (TAA) affiliated with the Cleveland Museum of Art, the fibers programs at the Cleveland Institute of Art and at Kent State University, and the Firelands Association for the Visual Arts, home of The Artist as Quiltmaker exhibition. Several quilt artists from this region or in the area, such as Judith Greene Albert, Susan Schroeder, and Peg Spaeth, were quite well known and actively exhibiting, but turned to other pursuits during the 1980s.

Two of the region's artists, JoAnn Giordano and Petra Soesemann, have spent their careers in academia. Both feel disconnected from the core of the "quilt world" because they have found their circle of support in a broader academic setting. Through their travels and their educational experiences both have been exposed to a wide range of media, and have a unique approach to their work in textiles. Through their exhibiting and teaching, however, they both have made a lasting contribution to the future of the field: young art school graduates.

JoAnn Giordano

JoAnn Giordano was born in Newark, New Jersey, in 1949. Her grandfather, an Italian immigrant, worked as a tailor, while her grandmother did the finishing work. She grew up seeing them working with their hands, cutting, manipulating, and stitching fabrics to create beautiful handmade garments. Although her mother did not sew, given the influence of her grandparents' artistry, it comes as no surprise that JoAnn would later create much of her artwork in the form of wearables.

JoAnn was raised Catholic, and from that experience was primarily influenced by the rituals and pageantry of the church. Growing up in the 1950s, she was sensitive to the constraints she perceived in women's lives, and as she grew into adulthood she sought alternatives to life as a housewife raising children.

Giordano graduated in 1971 from the Rhode Island School of Design with a BFA in interior architecture, having spent her senior year studying in Rome. She also studied batik and dyeing with a Japanese instructor in New York City, and became intrigued with the possibilities of working with textiles. She joined the Surface Design Association (SDA) and attended their first conference in 1977. That same year she received a scholarship and went to Purdue University to study for a master's degree in textiles. Giordano "got serious about textiles" while at Purdue. "Textile [work] has always been outside the mainstream. . . . I'm interested in narrative more than anything. The medium, materials, technique . . . it all depends on what I want to say."[27]

Cosmic Fantasy Jacket, 1980. JoAnn Giordano. 19" x 44". Silk screen printed on silk, handmade frog closures. (Folkwear Chinese Jacket pattern.) Clothing has the potential to change the wearer's mood: to elevate the spirit, to amuse, to create magic. This is the role the artist hopes her wearables serve. Photo courtesy of the artist.

Giordano has been influential because she has used mixed media techniques in wearables and quilts, fabric collage, wirecloth, and sculpture throughout her career. Despite her soft-spoken manner, her soul finds a voice in her richly layered narrative work, where she speaks about lovers and relationships, and confronts political issues related to the role of women and the environmental movement.

With two master's degrees, in fibers and in textiles (the second earned at Cranbrook), she is an expert in surface design techniques. She came to Ohio in the 1980s to replace the late Wenda von Weise in the fibers program at CIA. After a few years, she began teaching in the fibers department at Kent State. Like Miriam Schapiro and other feminist artists of her time, the influence of Giordano's work is in its message. For artists, her work offers carte blanche permission to pour out their souls.

Petra Soesemann

Petra Soesemann was born in 1953 in Göttingen, Germany, and immigrated with her family to Wooster, Ohio, in 1955. Growing up in Wooster, she was familiar with traditional quilts, and says she was interested in being an artist her entire life: "I loved sewing. It's the very first thing I learned as far as 'making' processes . . . [but in my artwork] I was bound and determined not to do anything that had any idea of domesticity attached to it. . . . Maybe that speaks to the times . . . you wanted to find a way to honor this tradition, to respect it and keep it alive, and on the other hand, going 'Oh my God . . . quilts.'"[28]

Although Soesemann was a sculpture major at CIA, she took some fiber classes and met Wenda von Weise, who was also a student there at the time. While finishing her MFA on scholarship at the Art Institute of Chicago in the late 1970s, she began working with textiles, but privately, she recalls. "When I started making quilts, it never occurred to me to go get a book on how to do that. . . . I just started sewing. . . . In the beginning I pretty much called them quilts. They're not constructed in the proper way."[29] After graduating in 1980, she began entering exhibitions, and showed in two Quilt Nationals during the decade. Her strong interest in landscape and the environment underlies a body of work related to patterning and light. To that is added the interaction of sheer fabrics, inspired by a Fulbright Scholarship and a year of study in Peru, where she was seduced by the "weightless and delicate" textile shrouds she discovered there.

Soesemann began teaching in various universities in 1985, and came to CIA in 1999 as chair of the

Sketchbook and fabric sketches. Petra Soesemann. Like many artists, Soesemann uses her journal as a sketchbook, recording impressions, drawings, and ideas inspired by her surroundings. These drawings and fabric sketches are created with sheer paper and fabrics, allowing the artist to see a mock-up of her ideas. Photo by John Seyfried.

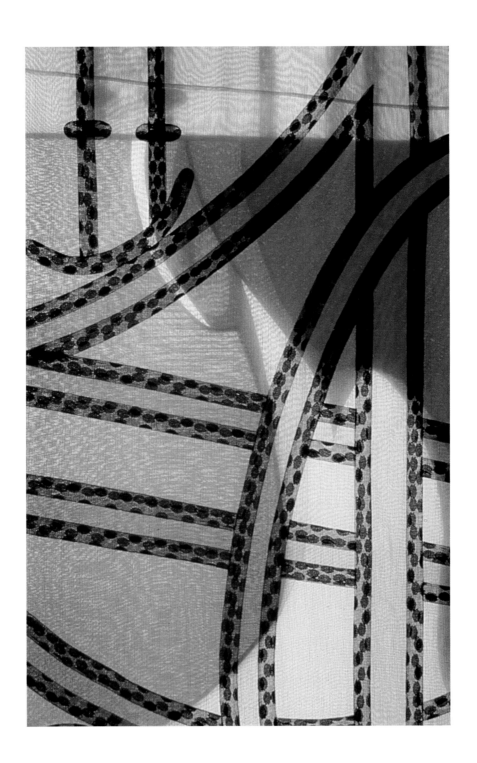

Great ideas are really a dime a dozen. The trick is [knowing] when you have a good idea. One thing I've never forgotten—an idea is very fragile; it has to be nurtured.

—Petra Soesemann, interview, 2004

Foundations Program. She has continued to experiment in her work, crossing the boundaries of the medium, collaborating on artists' books, and working on ever larger fabric constructions and installations. One such piece that won Best of Show in Quilt National '95 illustrates an early use of her layering techniques. The jurors said of her work: "In deliberation . . . one question was often raised: why is this a quilt and not a painting or a tapestry? [Soesemann's] piece pushes the boundaries of the quilt form to produce subtle and mysteriously transparent images that are uniquely suited to her idea. Her references to movement, solid mass, evolution, travel, and basic humanity are pulled together in a way that is possibly only with a double-sided quilt format."[30] Soesemann is a pioneering artist in the exploration of the nature of fabric itself and the new fibers technology, such as the current development of "smart fabric." As it has throughout history, the development of new types of fabrics will continue to inspire artists to find new ways to use them in their artwork.

MEN/WOMEN, Chapter 1: The Gambler (detail), 1994. Petra Soesemann. 75" x 76". Natural and synthetic fabric, direct hand and machine appliqué, fused, hand-quilted. This two-sided piece emphasizes Soesemann's artistry in using the veiling effects of layered sheer fabrics interacting with available light to convey her message. The shorthand encryption reads: "Women veil their egos the way men mask their emotions." Collection of John M. Walsh III.

Elizabeth Cave

Although Elizabeth Cave was born in Chicago in 1924, the Cave family moved to Ohio in 1933, Elizabeth says, "because my family lost everything in the Depression years, and my father's sister lived in Mansfield."[31] In 1941, she left for college at DePauw University, and then the war started: "The outbreak of World War II greatly altered the lives of those in my generation. After two years of college, [I] came home [and] went to work." In the mid-1960s, she ultimately earned a degree in painting from Ashland College, and spent the rest of her career teaching art.

Cave was active in the formation of the Mansfield Art Center, often teaching and volunteering there since the late 1960s. She remembers director emeritus Daniel Butts fondly: "He was our first director . . . [and] has been very supportive of quilt-making. During his tenure . . . he hosted two shows of Art Quilt Network members, plus another called 'The Dishtowel Quilt Project' put together by [Susan] Shie. All were great successes, and one of the AQN shows pulled in more visitors than any exhibit up until that time."

After seeing a collection of antique Amish quilts in the late 1970s, Cave says, "I put away my paints and bought Beth Gutcheon's book, *The Patchwork Primer* and began trying to make a small quilt. I still have that first one, and it is a humbling experience to get it out and look at it." She continued to make quilts, joined a local guild for a time, and had her first exhibition in 1982 at Ashland's Coburn Gallery. She exhibited in the inaugural Artist as Quiltmaker show in 1984, and by 1985 her work was shown in Quilt National. In the mid-1980s, she met Nancy Crow when she signed up for a workshop, and soon became part of the network of art quilters in the state and an early member of the Art Quilt Network.

In 1989, she experienced a personal breakthrough in her work with *Thunder Moon,* the first work she created incorporating painting, embellishments, and embroidery. Retired from teaching, Cave remains quite proud of an art program she began at a large prison just outside Mansfield. "It no longer exists, but *The Shawshank Redemption* was filmed there. Even though I was a volunteer, I had a badge and went in alone. The class grew to twenty-three very talented men, all the room could hold, with a waiting list. I talked the State of Ohio into providing paints and brushes, and we made our own stretchers of lumber from the furniture factory and 'canvas' of denim left over from the clothing factory. . . . I'd like to be remembered by the art students who passed through my classes. When they see a famous painting, need to mix a certain color or do a perspective drawing, I'd like them to think, 'Hey, we learned that in art!'"

Thunder Moon, 1989. Elizabeth Cave. 41" x 72". Pieced cotton, painted, embroidered, embellished, hand- and machine-quilted. This piece was a turning point for Cave, a painter by training, and she has continued to develop her quilts in this manner. The curved top of the piece, she says, is "a device I later gave up because of hanging difficulties." Photo courtesy of the artist.

Susan Shie

Susan Shie was born in Wooster, Ohio, in 1950, and has lived in Wayne County most of her life. Of the four children in her family, she and a brother were born with albinism, a genetic condition in which there is little or no pigment in the eyes, skin, or hair. Eyesight is often affected, and those with the condition are light-sensitive. As a result, Shie recalls, "I couldn't go outside to play . . . it was too bright. I couldn't see the ball . . . couldn't go swimming. . . . I learned to entertain myself . . . early on just as a natural part of my life, and my mother was sewing all the time."[32] By the time she was five, Susan had learned to sew to help pass the time.

She also loved to draw. Her parents made sure she always had art supplies and paper, sometimes accumulated junk mail or newsprint her mother collected from the *Wooster Daily Record* offices. Her

Artist Journals, Kent State Years, 1982. Susan Shie. Shie's journals are inseparable from her artwork; both contain stories, drawings, and ideas drawn from her daily life. Collection of the artist. Photo by John Seyfried.

dad even paid for her to take a three-year correspondence course in art, sacrificing to afford the six-hundred-dollar fee. Understandably, her disability affected her, at the very least because she always looked different. For nine years, she took a long bus ride every day to a special school program in Akron. What may have been a liability to some became for Susan the foundation of her personal strength and maverick personality. She was already different, so she never allowed herself to be dissuaded from the course of her ideas. Her disability gave her permission to "do her own thing."

An art student at Kent State University during the height of the Vietnam War, Shie was active in student protests and in creating art related to her political beliefs. "I think I'm alive because I dropped out of school and got married." Her work continued to evolve on the wings of the feminist and environmental movements, all the while serving as a forum for spiritual connection and healing. Shie finished her degree in painting at the College of Wooster in 1981. It was there that she began working on unstretched canvas. "I was getting upset, because my paintings were getting too big to move." She was living in town and unable to drive, so this presented difficulties. She asked her advisor if she could just roll up her paintings and transport them that way. "As soon as I started working on something that wasn't stretched, I realized, if it was a little thinner, I could stitch on this." She switched to working on a base of unbleached muslin.

She made another important discovery while working on her senior exhibition. As she, with her mother and other women as extra hands, embroidered the kimono-shaped hangings, the embroidery was so fine that visitors thought it was done by

Magic Show (detail), 1988. Susan Shie. Embroidered and embellished fabrics and stuffed shapes, hand-quilted. Shie's obsessively worked surfaces, filled with narrative text, symbols, and objects stitched and shaped into a whole, can cast a spell on viewers as they are invited into the artist's private world. Photo courtesy of the artist.

machine. "That was what made me realize I wanted to make my sewing funkier."

When art history professor Thalia Gouma-Peterson, whom Susan describes as "one of the first art historians who plugged into feminism," brought Miriam Schapiro to the College of Wooster for a residency, Schapiro and Shie developed a friendship that would continue through correspondence and later encounters while Shie was in graduate school at Kent State. Schapiro, a feminist artist and founder of the Pattern and Decoration Movement, is a champion of women's needlework, and played a substantial role in bringing the value of textiles onto the radar screen of the art world. During the residency, Shie recalls, "Miriam came around, and her big shtick was, all this stuff women are doing at home is art, and how come it's not showing up in our studio work?"

Shie finished her MFA in painting at Kent State in 1986, continuing with her narrative themes about everyday life. In graduate school, she learned that "artwork had to be original research; I have to do what hasn't been done before. . . . I write diaries, paint narrative images. I like to sew. . . . [My] diary quilt paintings embraced all these things at once." When her advisor at Kent saw the 1987 Quilt National prospectus in a magazine, he encouraged Shie to enter.

Folk art aesthetics and the counterculture find common ground in Susan Shie's artwork. She splashed onto the art quilt scene with her iconoclastic and diaristic quilt, *Neighborhood with Comet Scar,* Best of Show winner at Quilt National in 1987. In a *Fiberarts* article, Sandra Sider wrote of Shie's work, "Hippie embroidery from the 1960s, with large stitches and free-form symbolic images, has often resurfaced in Shie's narrative pieces. Shie asserts that the 'tribal' art of hippie embroidery is 'really at the root' of her art quilts."[33]

Shie's work is entirely individualistic and not easily categorized. It is too often poorly copied by admirers of her pioneering style. Her work lies outside the circles of both traditional painting and quilting. It reads as a personal diary, and until recently, was always constructed using small and portable finished units in a manner she invented. Although her work is often shaped, the richly layered, stuffed, and stitched components, as they are placed in the composition, create the individualistic shape called for in the piece, and are not planned in advance. When asked how she would like to be remembered, Shie responded thoughtfully: "In a room full of artists, I want people to know my work on sight. . . . The only people in art history books are the iconoclasts."

We each came in with our own style. I think it's much harder now for people to have their own style, because this is a ready-made movement, and there's too much eye candy.

—Susan Shie, interview, 2004

LEATHER ARTIST JAMES ACORD, Susan Shie's long-time friend and husband, was born in Fairfield, Illinois, in 1953. Primarily self-taught, Acord began working in leather in 1977 and was a "former protégé of Cleveland-area leather craftsman Bill Jones."[34] The couple met in Wooster and shared a studio at the Needle's Eye commune, Shie with Barnfire Pottery and Acord with Barnfire Leather. Acord started with custom orders only, creating everything from "custom fitted sandals to belts and wallets . . . vests and pants to motorcycle seats and saddlebags. Hats, handbags, wineskins, coats, gun holsters for cops."[35] Until she went back to school, Shie helped in the leather shop, creating custom coats and funky purses.

Acord began collaborating with Shie on her quilts in 1989, creating intricately tooled and airbrushed

The Girl Who Had to Wait Till She Was 21 to Own a Slinky (detail), 1992. Susan Shie and James Acord. The realism Acord is able to achieve in leather provides an effective contrast to Shie's iconic imagery. Photo courtesy of the artists.

animals, masks, and other embellishments related to the pieces. He learned to embroider the detailed narrative onto fabric, which he added to many pieces. He worked with Shie as they taught workshops in their home-based Turtle Art Camp and traveled with her to offer classes all over the world throughout the 1990s. When he decided to focus on his exquisite custom fly-fishing cases and bamboo rods in 1996, he gradually stepped back from the collaborations and now works independently.

The Millennium

A New Century of Art Quilts

In a 1989 *Fiberarts* article, Penny McMorris wrote, "Quiltmaking seems to be nearing a turning point. . . . Now, some of the best-known quiltmakers have a hard time holding onto enough work to exhibit. . . . The demand to see and show today's quilts has spread internationally. . . . Quilt popularity here and abroad continues to grow because people are still rediscovering quilts." She ended her article with an optimistic prediction: "Quiltmaking in the next decade promises to be as active and interesting as it has been in the 1980s."[1]

Indeed, growth continued throughout the 1990s and into the twenty-first century, and there are now reportedly more than twenty million quilters in the United States alone. Although no separate statistics for the makers of art quilts exist, there seems to be no sign of a slowdown, as established artists continue on their paths and new faces continue to appear. What is changing, however, is the orientation toward the field of art quilting evidenced by some established and many emerging artists. Curator and author Robert Shaw verified this trend in a recent interview: "As people work with . . . the idea of

quilting and the problems . . . they [are] defining in their work, some are calling their work 'mixed-media textiles' or just plain 'fiber art' because they . . . don't really see their work as fitting into the flow and tradition of quiltmaking."[2]

Art quilts have taken on new forms and are being made with new materials. New technologies have gradually become integrated into our daily lives. For those who work with textiles, technological advances have increased the number of available surfaces and affected virtually every artist working today. Improved dyes and dyeing techniques, as well as computers capable of scanning, manipulating, and printing imagery, have joined tools like airpens and computerized sewing machines that have enabled artists to incorporate new fabrics, materials,

You Are What You Eat I, 2001. Ruta Butkus Marino. 42" x 38". Collaged and appliquéd cotton, machine-quilted. In this series of sculptural quilts, Marino takes a humorous and perhaps critical stab at popular culture, creating each figure out of "food". The fabrics are collaged, appliquéd, and quilted before the figures are cut and rejoined with eating utensils. Photo courtesy of the artist.

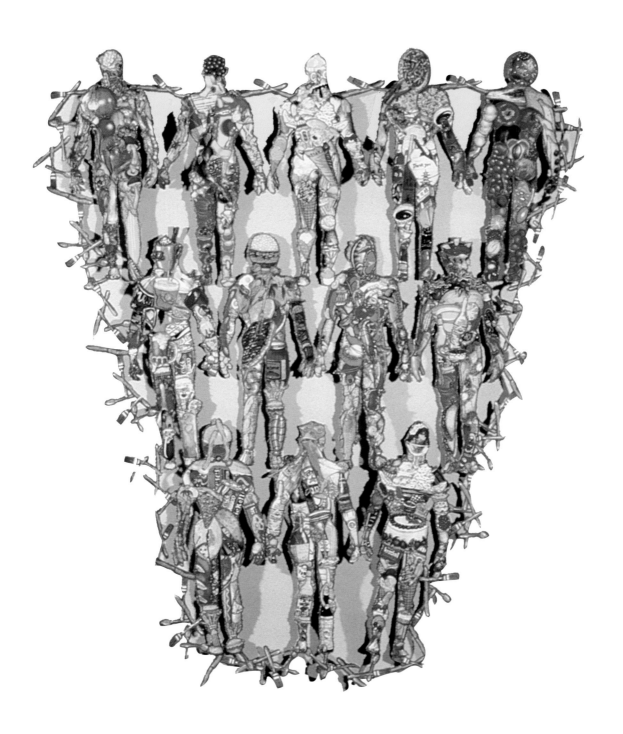

Evidence of the Un-sewn, #4 (detail), 2000. Clare Murray. In this series of work, the artist's quilt is deconstructed and the pieces, the evidence, reassembled and encased. The quilt as domestic object becomes a specimen, a diary of the artist's day-to-day responses to working with old pieces in this way. Photo courtesy of the artist.

and threads that would have previously been un-suited to handwork. Such developments have also allowed for the emergence of the sewing machine as a programmable drawing and writing tool.

Technology related to the continual experimentation with surface design techniques has had by far the greatest impact on the field, and that tendency will likely continue in the foreseeable future. As Michael James observes, "The aesthetic history of the patchwork quilt is inextricably linked to the history of the printed textile. Today, the advent of digital textile printing in the studios of contemporary quiltmakers . . . signals a sea change in how these artists . . . interact with the constructed textile surface. . . . It will significantly affect the way that imagery is created for and within the quilt surface . . . [and] will contribute to the ongoing transformation of the quilt medium."[3]

As the trend toward media crossover that began in the 1950s continues, many of today's quilt artists are using contemporary alternative materials and incorporating traditional assemblage and installation forms into their work. Generally speaking, however, the diversity of materials and techniques become, as Deborah Anderson expressed earlier, part of the grab bag of tools all artists use to create successful compositions consistent with their artistic goals. In most cases, what is important is not how the work is created, but rather how artists use these methods to convey their ideas.

Politics and the Natural Environment

Women have used needle and thread to express their political viewpoints throughout history. With no lack of subject matter or opinions in contemporary society, Ohio's quilt artists continue to make statements about the economy, the presidency, war, unemployment, damage to the environment, the status of women and minorities, even the Tiananmen Square massacres in China. This type of commentary often takes the form of visual storytelling. The role of artists in society is to reflect their ideas about the world back to the world. Political statements are often made when an artist is inspired by anger or a sense of responsibility to document and comment on society's current state of affairs.

Susan Shie has always stayed involved in her community, serving as president of the Wooster Food Co-op, teaching at the local art center, and organizing exhibits. In the late 1980s she reprised her role as an activist to close down a toxic medical waste incinerator scheduled to be built in Wooster. After attending a Greenpeace workshop, she returned home unsure how to integrate her anger and outrage with her belief in positive spiritual affirmation. The solution was revealed to her "like a

Back to Eden: A Green Quilt, 1989. Susan Shie and James Acord. 80" x 78". Fabric, paint, dye, leather, quartz crystals, beads, buttons, fish scales, three-dimensional appliquéd figures; hand-pieced, embroidered, painted, and quilted. The first ever Green Quilt, and the first collaboration between the artists, this quilt contains a central figure, Copper Woman, who carries the message, "Learn from the Animals; Return Our Earth to a Peaceable Kingdom." With two shrine doors that open and fourteen personal totem animals in leather, which flip over to reveal secret pockets, the work is irresistibly interactive. Collection of Darrel and Nancy Siebert.

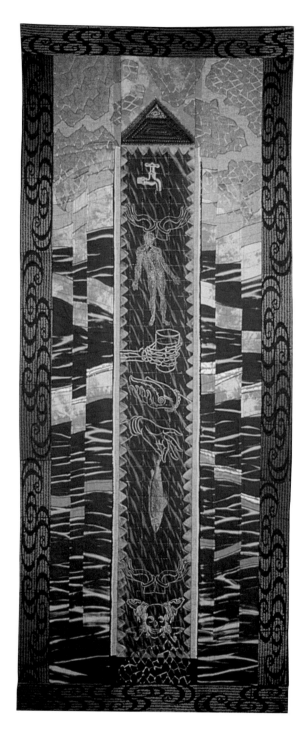

Water Prayer Rug, 1992. JoAnn Giordano. 34" x 83". Screen-printed, tie-dyed, discharged and appliquéd cotton, machine-quilted. Speaking directly to environmental issues, this piece uses imagery from aquatic life and human anatomy to remind us of the importance of water to all biological life. The border texture is composed of the names of toxic chemicals commonly found in drinking water. Photo courtesy of the artist.

message in a bottle" in her daily meditations: in 1987 Susan founded Green Quilts, a global environmental organization that invited participants to make quilts imbued with positive energy for the healing of the environment.[4] New York friend and artist Robin Schwalb maintained a slide registry, and Shie created a logo for labels affixed to the quilt backs. Hundreds of artists from all over the world created work to support the effort.

JoAnn Giordano's work, *Water Prayer Rug,* uses an ancient textile form, the prayer rug, to address her concerns about the environment by bringing attention to the global importance of water and its conservation in her composition. Terrie Hancock Mangat, in her unique narrative voice, has spoken out about the violence of terrorism (see page 30) and of war. In *Lake Superior Stick Bed* she combines quiltmaking with installation and assemblage traditions to create a commentary about pollution that the viewer can literally lie down on.

Akron artist Angela White creates what she calls Garbology, "the study of people and culture through what they throw away,"[5] and Living Sculpture, wearable garbage. Her work points a finger at our throwaway society, and throws viewers off guard by creating alluring, and often beautiful, artwork from

Lake Superior Stick Bed, 1996. Terrie Hancock Mangat. 80" x 45" x 42". Hand-appliquéd, embroidered and embellished fabrics, paint, beach sticks. Hand-quilted by Sue Rule. This installation piece, shown in Quilt National '97, is an example of how the art quilt is expanding into other forms. Mangat says, "I gathered these sticks while walking the shore of Lake Superior, thinking about pollution and our water system. We have come dangerously close to destroying our home, the planet Earth. This bed (with the wolves peering out behind the sticks) represents the environmental bed we have made, and now must sleep in." Photo courtesy of the artist.

the accumulations of garbage she collects at dumps, on the streets, and anywhere else she finds it. As she collects, she maps out where she finds the garbage, creating narratives of the "unwanted, unused histories of everyday life." Because everyone creates trash, White feels that she connects with the people who have either tossed or lost what she collects, and through her art connects them with one another, creating a new history.

Her work may appear politically motivated on the surface, and there is an environmental aspect to it, but she finds her personal meaning and motivation in the "stuff" itself. She was attracted to and became obsessed with reclaiming the personal histories of cast-off objects in 2000 when, over the course of the summer, her brother, his wife, and their baby were all killed in car accidents. She recalls the painful time: "Before that I was making work with materials that didn't have any real personal meaning. . . . After he died I went through all of his belongings. . . . It really made me think differently. . . . I [began to] think more about the history of the objects."

For *Fast Food Quilt*, White collected garbage from the Cuyahoga River and stitched it together into a quilt. Viewers are lured into the piece by the bright colors and unusual materials, visible even from a distance. Up close, the all-too-familiar

Angela White. The concern for the environment that came into prominence in the 1970s has been passed on to another generation. Emerging Akron artist Angela White, who calls herself a "garbologist," searches a dump for materials to recycle in her artwork. Photo by Jody Hawk.

brand names of contemporary consumer society stare back at us, a time capsule of sorts, as we wonder how a work so delicate and beautiful could have been constructed from the detritus. Similarly, in *Akron City Quilt*, made from rubber car parts collected at a dump, White asks the viewer to reconsider a quilt's traditional purpose.

Akron City Quilt (detail), 2001. Angela White. 48" x 88". Found and layered rubber car parts, home-made grommets. White's work is focused on the materials. She selects the form in which they will be presented based on what experience she hopes to evoke for the viewer. This quilt creates a new history from the dozens of cast-off rubber car parts, and represents the lives of those who owned each of these cars. Photo courtesy of the artist.

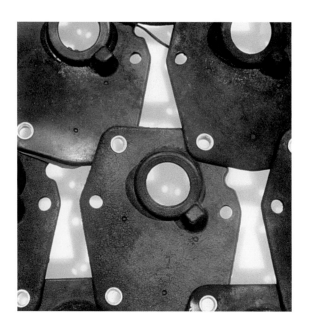

Fast Food Quilt, 2001. Angela White. 60" x 108". Gathered, documented, and layered trash from the Cuyahoga River, hand-stitched. White, whose family has a history of quiltmaking, has been sewing since she was twelve. She used these skills to construct this work: a quilt made of trash. By hanging the work on a wall to confront viewers, White hoped to encourage the audience to think differently about the quilt and the materials from which it is made. Photo by John Seyfried.

Fast Food Quilt (detail), 2001. Angela White. Here, as in an old scrap quilt, White uses common materials that are approachable and understandable by the viewer. In the same way that a dress scrap was recognized in a cherished scrap quilt, here viewers recognize the familiar in scraps of trash presented in the quilt, now evolved from its original function. Photo by John Seyfried.

In her work, Wenda von Weise expressed her deep concern about the deterioration of the environment, especially as urban and suburban development began to threaten rural areas. Using photographs she took to document her surroundings, she applied silk-screening techniques extensively to create deconstructed landscapes, visual maps of a sort, to illustrate her ideas (see pages 15–17).

Interesting visual commonalities to von Weise's work appear in the work of Athens artist John Lefelhocz. Both artists often reference the quilt-making tradition while utilizing the layering capabilities of the technologies available to them to evoke their contemporary visions of their narrative landscapes. Lefelhocz uses found alternative materials extensively. He integrates his materials so well

Fabricated Landscapes: Four Furrows (and detail, above), 1978. Wenda von Weise. 67" x 72". Photographic silk screen on silk, hand-quilted. After years of exploring photographs of textures found in nature, von Weise began incorporating these images into her dreamlike landscapes, saying, "Indeed, once I had identified texture as a factor I realized that it was texture which had drawn me to the fiber field in the first place." Works in her *Fabricated Landscapes* series are structured like the traditional straight furrows quilt pattern. In this work, the layered imagery of the grass in the furrows is seen from two perspectives. Photo courtesy the von Weise estate.

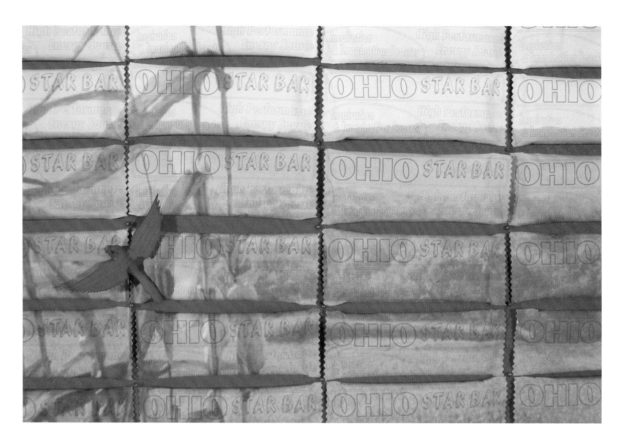

in the composition that they become visible only at close range. He says, "There's an Appalachian culture here, where you . . . make what you've got work."[6] In *Ohio Star Bar: Inspiration on the Wing*, Lefelhocz brilliantly references both traditional quilts and landscape with imagery created in part on the computer. He says, "From a distance it looks like a traditional quilt, and I really enjoy that. . . . I like including that lineage because it means something now, and it's going to mean something entirely different down the road."[7]

Ohio Star Bar/Inspiration on the Wing (and detail, above), 2003. John Lefelhocz. 58" x 65". Cotton, cotton duck, tulle net, printed paper, feathers, foam. Born in Pittsburgh in 1967, Lefelhocz moved to Ohio in 1977. An avid cyclist and a self-taught artist creating assemblage and sculpture, he was inspired to make quilts by a visit to Quilt National '97. John's quilts debuted in Quilt National '99. In his early work, John says, "I was hand-stitching with dental floss through window screening; now, I'm using machine quilting every now and then." John's *Ohio Star Bar* represents his own special mix of energy and imagination and evokes Ohio's landscape and the Ohio Star quilt pattern. Quotes written on the cardinals include the following: "I don't know what you could say about a day in which you have seen four beautiful sunsets" (John Glenn); and "If we did all the things we are capable of, we would literally astound ourselves" (Thomas A. Edison). Photo courtesy of the artist.

The Aesthetics of Abstraction

For some artists, the tools of composition are the focus. In the case of Nancy Crow, color is at the forefront of her artistic concerns, as she continues to create cutting-edge abstract work. As Paul J. Smith notes, "Nancy Crow was a pioneer in developing a new aesthetic for the modern quilt. . . . One of the strongest aspects of [her] work is her exceptional talent in manipulating color. . . . These visual fantasies combine richness of fabric, meticulous craftsmanship, and a strong graphic order. Their powerful presence reflects her deep sensitivity to the beauty of life."[8]

In the late 1980s, Crow reached an impasse in her work and was close to quitting. "All my work was mirror-imaged and symmetrical. I knew that I could never really go on if I didn't figure out a way to get out of this. . . . 1990 was a pivotal year."[9] She was inspired to rethink her approach after seeing the improvisational method of Anna Williams, a self-taught African American quiltmaker from Louisiana. Bringing her own aesthetic concerns to solving problems in her work, by 1993 Nancy had worked for years learning to "memory cut" by teaching her hand to draw directly on the fabric with a blade. This work opened up a new series of intuitive exploration for her.

Oberlin artist Britt Friedman creates lyrical abstract quilts that often stem from her interest in photography. In *Current Events* she evokes the movement of waves in an abstract painterly fashion using cutting-edge technology to create her imagery.

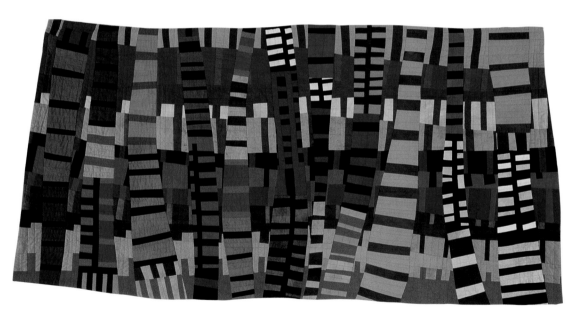

Constructions #38, 2000. Nancy Crow. 77" x 38". Cotton, some hand-dyed by the artist, machine-pieced, hand-quilted by Marla Hattabaugh. Crow's approach to her dynamic asymmetrical compositions is proof of the artist's commitment to continuous growth while exploring her subject matter in great depth. Her *Constructions* series, while visually abstract, is inspired by her studio surroundings: a beautiful barn. Photo by John Seyfried.

Current Events, 2003. Britt Friedman. 48" x 60". Cotton, paint, dye. A native of Sweden and a clinical psychologist, Friedman is known for her dedication to discovery in her work. Also a painter, she began making quilts in the late 1980s. The abstract use of color and pattern in her quilts reflects her love of painting, and she describes her use of fabric as "seeing the fabric strips as brushstrokes." Photo courtesy of the artist.

Both with the images and words the works read as a personal diary of a trip, experiences or feelings. . . . One feels a bit voyeuristic, as if looking into their lives and essences of existence by reading their personal diaries.

—Lynn Lewis Young, *Art/Quilt Magazine*, 1995

Monkeyshrines, 2000. Andrea Stern. 60" x 28". Appliquéd cotton, found fabric and found objects, hand-beaded and embroidered, pennies, paint. Hand-quilted. Stern constructed this work, made while she nursed her newborn, in small units for ease of completion. The artist says, "Both the dress and the monkey were outlined with quotes from Psalms and Darwin, respectively. I found it interesting how Darwin's writing sounded as if it could have come from the Bible." When viewed from a distance, the artist's work creates a sense of longing and nostalgia. Photo by John Seyfried.

Telling Tales

Narrative storytelling in quilts has a long history. Narrative work is often rendered with appliqué or appliqué-like techniques. In narrative compositions, the use of language adds an additional layer of interest, as in Susan Shie's diaristic quilts. Although words are not an ingredient necessary to this genre, language itself has become a popular surface design strategy. In a *Fiberarts* article, Jan Janeiro wrote, "The combination of text and image—once thought to be anathema to the . . . creation of visual art— has seen a tremendous contemporary upsurge of development in all art media."[10]

Chauncey artist Andrea Stern's work shows the influence of the embellishment movement, inherent to the narrative style of artists such as Terrie Hancock Mangat and Susan Shie, but Stern is able to transcend the pervasive influences and make her own statement. The imagery in *Monkeyshrines*, like most of her work, evokes an unspoken sense of yearning, which is consistent with the artist's attempts to capture memories in her work. The use of a found antique child's dress creates an eerie feeling of loss.

Cleveland area artists Sharon Bell and Sandy Shelenberger have both worked with text in their narrative quilts, but in different ways. Bell, influenced by Japanese culture, finds a Zenlike spiritual peace in her work. *Numbers* uses sumi ink and is, according to the artist, "influenced by simplicity. I try to keep my work minimal, relying on the tactile surface to generate interest."[11] Shelenberger's *Black and Blue #1: Resistance* appears to air dirty laundry with large words visible from a distance, but abstracted at close range.

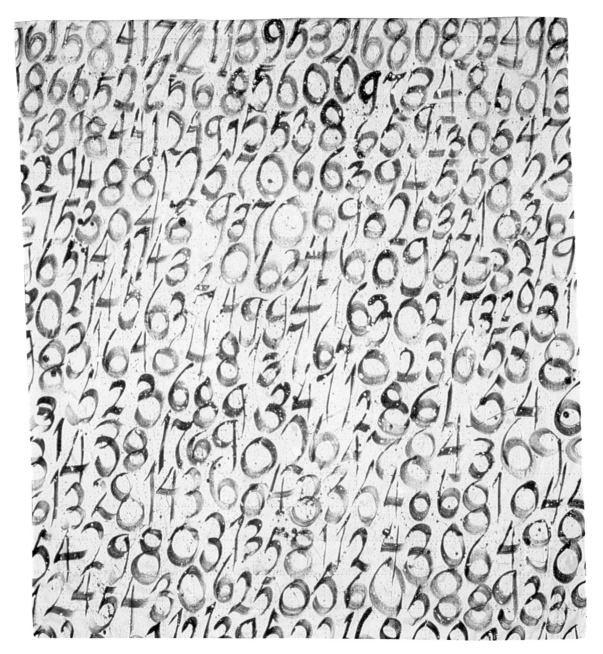

Numbers, 2001. Sharon Bell. 50" x 55". Whole cloth, paint, sumi ink, hand-quilted. This work is one of seven in the artist's *Book* series, visual interpretations of biblical titles: Genesis, Deuteronomy, Exodus, Judges, Kings, Numbers, and Apocalypse (Revelations). Photo courtesy of the artist.

Black and Blue #1: Resistance, 2003. Sandy Shelenberger. 25.5" x 25.5". Airbrushed and painted cotton, machine-quilted. Part of a series, the work reads like a jumbled puzzle, creating an appealing graphic composition based on words. By limiting her color use and working with stark contrasts, the artist creates a jarring composition full of movement, enhanced by the texture of the quilting. Photo courtesy of the artist.

Reach for the Stars, 2004. Cynthia Lockhart. 51" x 67". Cottons, blends, rayon, taffeta, lamé, leather, suede, metallic cording, braid and fabrics. Machine-pieced, appliquéd, embellished, hand-stitched French bias. This piece expresses the raw and joyful energy the artist utilizes to go for her dreams. Intricate dressmaking details add to the surface interest of the composition. Lockhart is a professor at the University of Cincinnati, teaching courses to fashion design students, among others. Photo by Jay Yocis.

Laws According to Which Water Flows (detail), 1997. Susan Krueger. Hand-made felt, wax resist, discharge, dye, embroidered, quilted. "My influence for *Laws* was seeing a small mola . . . of what seemed to be a mythological figure, the centaur . . . but on closer inspection, two breasts could be seen!" The artist often uses intricate embroidery to tell her stories in fiber. Photo by David Hampshire.

Cincinnati artist Cynthia Lockhart draws upon her career in fashion design, creating unique, shaped narrative pieces reminiscent of sewing pattern pieces. Using familiar dressmaking materials and techniques, the artist brings a lifetime of experience to her explorations in quiltmaking.

Susan Krueger, of Bowling Green, Ohio, thinks of her work as fiber collage. She often uses alternative materials, such as brilliantly dyed and felted wool fleece, to create her narrative compositions. She uses various surface design techniques, such as batik or discharge, and creates a foundation fabric on which she appliqués and quilts. In *Laws According to Which Water Flows,* she makes extensive use of embroidery, which "has a historical connection to countless anonymous women. This makes me feel like part of one big family."[12]

Conclusion

THE STORY OF THE EMERGENCE AND EVOLUTION of the art quilt movement in Ohio reveals the profound and lasting impact of Ohio's artists in both national and international arenas. As this story ends, it begins anew, with new artists, new artwork, and new ways of exploring the seemingly inexhaustible quilt form, assuring that the medium will continue to develop and evolve in both predictable and unforeseeable ways in the coming years. Every contribution by every known Ohio quilt artist has left evidence of the vibrancy and commitment Ohioans have made to the state of art quilting. We look forward to the continued contributions of Ohio's artists.

The Art Quilt Arrives, or Does It?

Quilt National's success in bringing art quilts into the limelight inspired Penny McMorris and the late Michael Kile to build on its accomplishments. In 1986, just ten years after the first exhibition at Bowling Green and seven short years after the debut of Quilt National, they held an exhibition of the leading artists of the time and published *The Art Quilt*, the first book to present a well-researched and scholarly approach to the evolution of the medium.[1] Collaborating on this seminal book, McMorris and Kile coined the term "art quilt" to describe the new work being created. In the transition of terminology from "new" to "contemporary" to "wall" to "innovative," the term "art quilt" said it all, and was soon universally applied. As Penny McMorris says in Robert Shaw's later book, also called *The Art Quilt*, "Michael and I were talking on the phone one night about what to call the book and exhibition we were working on, going through all kinds of possible variations such as 'Quilted Art,' 'The Art of the Quilt,' 'The Quilter's Art,' etc. When we said the words 'Art Quilt' it felt right, as the briefest titles usually do. Up until then we had never heard the term used; since then I've come across it used back at the turn of the [twentieth] century."[2]

This terminology represents only the tip of the iceberg in the ongoing art *vs.* craft debate. Today the term "art quilt" is almost universally despised, a

Monet for Nothing/Insufficient Postage (detail), 2000. John Lefelhocz. 44" x 43". Fabric, nylon mesh, beads, copper wire, paper, clear plastic transparencies. Lefelhocz's use of the layering of imagery and text on fabric, achieved with the assistance of today's technology, aptly illustrates the sophistication of surface design achieved by today's artists. The artwork was part of the traveling exhibition Quilt 21: American Art Quilts for the 21st Century. Photo courtesy of the artist.

term which Penny herself says "no longer serves."[3] In an article for the *New Art Examiner,* craft critic Matthew Kangas wrote, "No matter how much we may wish the art versus craft debate to go away, it never will; it is a central aesthetic question which provokes debate. . . . Perhaps the fine arts world would prefer craft artists to agree on a single definition of crafts, simply because it would be easier, as was once the case, to dismiss them as irrelevant."[4]

An article published in the prestigious *Wall Street Journal* in 2002 perhaps reflects most poignantly the ongoing struggle artists in this medium face. In a blanket criticism of museum quilt exhibitions, author Brooks Barnes dismisses art quilts as "beaux-arts blankies" while bemoaning the fact that "even 'fiber arts' . . . are showing up in big museums at a time when, coincidentally or not, budgets are at their tightest in a decade." He ends his column with a call to arms, "But even the folks in the art world think museums should raise the bar, if only a bit."[5] Clearly, art quilts have a long way to go in securing broad-based respect in the traditional art world.

In discussing the struggles faced by artists, more than two decades ago Nancy Crow said, "I think every artist who succeeds . . . has some ability to keep moving forward in the face of constant obstacles . . . emotional, mental, financial, physical whatever, and that is what sets them apart from all the ones who have tried and quit, and from those who always talk about trying . . . but never get beyond the talking stage. Entering one's studio is the same as confronting oneself. . . . It takes courage to be an artist, and one usually pays a price."[6]

What is wonderful about the process of creating is that all artists approach problems from a uniquely different place, bringing their own passion and experience to their work, and confronting their own demons. As Nancy Crow intuited, good ideas seem to come when something is at risk. At the very least, the risk of rejection is always present. Despite these risks, both personal and public, for the past forty years, Ohio's quilt artists have been breaking new ground. We are grateful for their legacy.

Hero Series (detail), 2006. Gayle Pritchard. 24" x 30". Image
transfers, found objects, embroidery, painted, appliqued,
hand-quilted. This is the third in the *Hero Series,* begun as a
way to commemorate her father, Neil Robert Vickery, and to
find healing after his sudden death in 1992. Pritchard made
her first quilt in 1973. Photo by Chris Pritchard.

Quilts Illustrated

Katrina Blues (detail), 2005. Susan Shie. 45" x 75.5". Airpen painting on cotton, overpainting, drawing, writing. Machine-quilted, hand-bound. This quilt was being created as Hurricane Katrina worked its way from Florida to New Orleans, and represents the artist's response to the devastation. Shie's work evolved from painting to obsessively embellished quilts; her recent work, while continuing her diaristic style, has become pared down, returning to her roots in painting with the addition of more writing to replace the embellishment. Photo courtesy of the artist.

$\mathcal{N}otes$

Preface

1. The complete list of jurors for the Artist as Quilt-maker exhibition is as follows: 1984/I: Penny McMorris; 1986/II: H. Daniel Butts III; 1988/III: Judi Warren Blaydon; 1990/IV: Terrie Hancock Mangat; 1992/V: Nancy Crow; 1994/VI: Penny McMorris; 1996/VII: Jan Myers-Newbury; 1998/VIII: Risë Nagin; 2000/IX: Susan Shie; 2002/X: Clare Murray; 2004:/XI: Invitational celebration and "Pathways and Perspectives" Symposium; 2006/XII: Linda Fowler.

The Groundwork for a Quilt Revolution

1. Penny McMorris and Michael Kile, *The Art Quilt* (San Francisco: Quilt Digest Press, 1986), 23.

2. Roderick Kiracofe, *The American Quilt: A History of Cloth and Comfort 1750–1950* (New York: Clarkson Potter, 1993), 5.

3. Carol Boram-Hays, *Bringing Modernism Home: Ohio Decorative Arts, 1890–1960* (Athens: Ohio University Press in conjunction with Columbus Museum of Art, 2005), 53. This book is an excellent reference for the history and influence of Ohio craft artists in the media discussed.

4. Patsy Orlofsky and Myron Orlofsky, *Quilts in America* (New York: Abbeville, 1992), 88.

5. Valerie S. Rake, "A Thread of Continuity: Quiltmaking in Wayne County, Ohio, Mennonite Churches, 1890s–1990s," *Uncoverings: The Research Papers of the American Quilt Study Group* 20 (1999): 32, 33.

6. Lloyd E. Herman, *Art That Works: Decorative Arts of the Eighties Crafted in America* (Seattle: University of Washington Press, 1990), 15.

7. Rose Slivka, "The Art/Craft Connection: A Personal, Critical, and Historical Odyssey," in *The Eloquent Object*, ed.

Marcia Manhart and Tom Manhart (Seattle: University of Washington Press for the Philbrook Museum of Art, Tulsa, OK, 1987), 76.

8. Boram-Hays, *Bringing Modernism Home,* 85, 86.

9. *Craft Horizons,* later renamed *American Craft,* began publication in 1941. *Fiberarts* began publication in 1976.

10. Slivka, "The Art/Craft Connection," 76, 77.

11. Robert Shaw, interviewed by Sunita Patterson, "The Art Quilt in 2003," *Fiberarts,* November/December 2003, 37.

12. Grace Glueck, "They're Shoofly and Crazy, Man," *New York Times,* Art Notes, June 27, 1971, D24.

13. Lois Martin, "The Making of Quilts, The Maker of Quilts," *American Craft Magazine,* June/July 1995, 32.

14. Jonathan Holstein, *The Pieced Quilt: An American Design Tradition* (New York: Galahad Books, 1973), 115.

15. Ibid., 187n4.

16. Patricia Mainardi, *Quilts: The Great American Art* (San Pedro, CA: Miles & Weir, 1978), 46, 47, 49. Article originally written for the *Feminist Art Journal.*

17. Bonnie Leman, "What's New—and News—In Quilting," *Quilter's Newsletter Magazine,* September 1971, 3.

18. Bonnie Leman, "What's New—and News—In Quilting," *Quilter's Newsletter Magazine,* February 1974, 3.

19. The exhibition was at the Akron Art Institute from February 10 through March 18, 1973, as reorganized by the Smithsonian Institution Traveling Exhibit Series (SITES).

20. For a complete history of the Whitney exhibition, which was reassembled and shown in 1991 by the Kentucky Quilt Project, see Jonathan Holstein, *Abstract Design in American Quilts: A Biography of an Exhibition* (Louisville: Kentucky Quilt Project, 1991).

21. *Quilter's Newsletter Magazine* published a rave review by Lee Hale. Hinting at the dearth of resource materials available at the time, Hale wrote: "The publication of a brand new book on modern quilting is a cause for celebration . . .

because it happens so seldom." *Quilter's Newsletter Magazine,* September 1971, 14.

22. Jean Ray Laury, *Quilts and Coverlets: A Contemporary Approach* (New York: van Nostrand Reinhold, 1970), 12–13.

23. *Surface Design Journal* began publication in 1977, joining *Quilter's Newsletter Magazine* (1969) and *Fiberarts* (1976).

24. Lloyd E. Herman and Matthew Kangas, *Tales and Traditions: Storytelling in Twentieth-Century American Craft* (Seattle: University of Washington Press, 1993), 36.

25. Alice Echols, "Women's Liberation and Sixties Radicalism," in *The Sixties: From Memory to History,* ed. David Farber (Chapel Hill: University of North Carolina Press, 1998), 151.

26. Marcia Manhart and Tom Manhart, "The Widening Arcs: A Personal History of a Revolution in the Arts," in *The Eloquent Object,* ed. Marcia Manhart and Tom Manhart (Seattle: University of Washington Press for the Philbrook Museum of Art, Tulsa, OK, 1987), 41.

27. Nancy Crow, unpublished interview with the author, Baltimore, Ohio, August 8, 2004.

28. Penny McMorris, "Quilting—A Reminiscence," *Lady's Circle Patchwork Quilts,* March 1986, 68.

29. Penny McMorris, unpublished interview with the author, May 24, 2004.

30. Helen Cullinan, "Unconventionally Suited: Arts Gallery Chief Puts Business Past to Good Use," *Cleveland Plain Dealer,* March 4, 1990, 2-H.

31. Herman and Kangas, *Tales and Traditions,* 44, 45.

32. Michael James, "The Digital Quilt," *Fiberarts,* November/December 2003, 26–31.

33. For a history of the project and detailed information about each block, see Bobbie Carlson, *A Patchwork Guide to Oberlin: The Oberlin Quilt* (Oberlin, OH: Press of the Times, 1976) or Adele Gittler, "Love-Letter in Thread: Quilt Captures Spirit of Oberlin," *Elyria (Ohio) Chronicle-Telegram,* May 19, 1974, C-1.

34. Carolyn Balducci, editor, and Judi Warren, design and layout, *The Maumee Quilt,* educational brochure.

35. McMorris, "Quilting—A Reminiscence," 30, 31, 68, 69.

36. Penny McMorris, "Quilter's Queries," *Quilter's Newsletter Magazine,* March 1976, 17.

37. Penny McMorris, unpublished interview with the author, May 24, 2004.

38. McMorris, "Quilting—A Reminiscence," 69. Exhibitor instructions provided by Elaine Plogman, Cincinnati, OH. Exhibition catalog from the collection of Penny McMorris, Bowling Green, Ohio.

39. McMorris, "Quilting—A Reminiscence," 69.

40. Helen Cullinan quoting Penny McMorris, "Quilt Guru Curates Oberlin Exhibit," *Cleveland Plain Dealer,* June 13, 1994, 3-E.

41. The term "art quilt" was invented by Penny McMorris and Michael Kile while they were writing *The Art Quilt,* originally published in 1986. Prior to that time, quilts made as an art form were referred to as "new quilts," "contemporary quilts," or "wall quilts."

Ohio's Art Quilt Pioneers

1. Barbara Brackman, "Rocky Road to Analysis," *Uncoverings: The Research Papers of the American Quilt Study Group,* 25 (2004): 8.

2. Places to See Quilts, *Quilter's Newsletter Magazine,* August 1972, 23.

3. In her movingly personal book, Nancy Crow thanks "Danny Butts," among others, for "encouraging my career." *Nancy Crow, Quilts and Influences* (Paducah, KY: American Quilter's Society, 1990), 252.

4. Nancy Crow, "Quilting: The Development of Art Quilts," *Fiberarts,* January/February 1990, 45.

5. Ford von Weise, unpublished interview with the author, March 29, 2005.

6. Ibid.

7. Charles von Weise, unpublished interview with the author, March 25, 2005.

8. Wenda von Weise, "Photoprinted Quilts," *Quilting II,* hosted by Penny McMorris, WBGU-TV, Bowling Green, OH, 1982.

9. Wenda von Weise, *Artists in Residence,* NOVA series hosted by Dennis Barrie for the Archives of American Art, Smithsonian Institution, Washington, DC, February 14, 1984.

10. Ibid.

11. For an excellent article about Rauschenberg's groundbreaking printmaking techniques, see Donald H. Karshan, "Robert Rauschenberg," *Art in America,* January/February 1971, 48.

12. Charles von Weise, unpublished interview with the author, March 25, 2005. Wenda von Weise's expertise in incorporating photographic imagery onto fabric was eventually brought into CIA's curriculum, which now has a full silk-screen studio and allows for more focus on conceptual work in fiber and crossover between media, such as fiber and photography.

13. The Cleveland Museum of Art, then under the leadership of Frederic Allen Whiting, established the May Show in 1919. The juried mixed-media exhibition was hung annually until 1993 and showcased the work of Ohio artists. In addition to von Weise, Ohio quilt artists such as Nancy Crow, Gayle Pritchard, Fran Soika, Mirjana Ugrinov, and Ann Warren exhibited in the May Show. Cleveland Museum of Art history researched at www.clevelandart.org.

14. Robert Shaw, *The Art Quilt* (New York: Hugh Lauter Levin, 1997), 61.

15. Gwen-lin Goo was at that time head of the fiber department of the Cleveland Institute of Art; Lenore Davis, Terrie Hancock Mangat, and Jane Burch Cochran, all Kentucky artists, are traditionally included with the Ohio art quilt scene, due to their proximity to and interaction with the Cincinnati, Ohio, artists.

16. Paul J. Smith, Ruth Amdur Tanenhaus, and Jonathan Holstein, *The New American Quilt* (New York: Museum of Contemporary Crafts of the American Crafts Council, 1976), 3. Founded in 1956, the museum was renamed the American Craft Museum in 1986 and the Museum of Arts and Design in 2002.

17. Gerhardt Knodel was head of Cranbrook's fiber program from 1970 to 1996 and is the current director of the academy. Wenda's brother Howard, also a student at Cranbrook, recalls that Knodel pushed her hard during her graduate work.

18. Wenda von Weise, "The Exploration of Photographic Imagery in Quilt Making" (MFA thesis, Cranbrook Academy of Art, 1978), 20.

19. Von Weise, *Artists in Residence*. The term "vernacular glance" is defined by Brian O'Doherty: "The vernacular glance is what carries us through the city every day, a mode of almost unconscious, or at least divided, attention. . . . It's just interested in what's there. . . . It dispenses with hierarchies of importance, since they are constantly changing ac-cording to where you are and what you need." *American Masters: The Voice and the Myth* (New York: Ridge Press, Random House, 1973), 197–98.

20. Ford von Weise, unpublished interview with the author, March 29, 2005.

21. Mirjana Ugrinov, unpublished interview with the author, September 17, 2004.

22. Ibid. Curated by Eva Bradshaw, the Ohio Pioneers of the Art Quilt exhibition and symposium were held in Columbus, Ohio, in 2003.

23. Judi Warren Blaydon, unpublished interview with the author, September 21, 2004.

24. "Judi Warren—Artist," *Lady's Circle Patchwork Quilts*, March 1986, 16, 59.

25. Judi Warren Blaydon, unpublished interview with the author, September 21, 2004.

26. Judi Warren Blaydon, unpublished e-mail correspondence with the author, March 22, 2005.

27. Sally Vallongo, "Artist Quilts Memories of Japan," *Toledo Blade Magazine*, July 6, 1997, F-6.

28. Judi Warren Blaydon, "A Dialogue for Serious Quilters," Art Quilt Network Ohio, January 1987, unpublished tape recording courtesy of Tafi Brown.

29. "New Quilters Exhibition Reviews Quilt Design," Toledo Museum of Art news release, February 1978. The exhibition was held February 12 through March 19, 1978. Showing their work were Becky Becker, Doris Como, Marilyn Dubielak, Carol Dunlap, Helen Hense, Pam Leary, Mary Mallin, Sue Perry, Cyndie Rothbard, Carol Stanford, and Barbara Studer.

30. Judi Warren Blaydon participated in antiwar groups such as Another Mother for Peace and War Is Not Healthy for Children and Other Living Things, and was also a member of the Panel of American Women, a national civil rights organization.

31. Judi Warren Blaydon, March 22, 2005, unpublished e-mail correspondence with the author.

32. Judi Warren Blaydon, unpublished interview with the author, September 21, 2004.

33. Judi Warren Blaydon, lecture to the Quilter's Guild of Dallas, Texas, October 2, 1997, researched at www.reddawn. net/quilt/jwarren.htm.

34. Shaw, *Art Quilt*, 265.

35. Judi Warren Blaydon, *The Quilt: New Directions for an American Tradition,* Quilt National '83 catalog (Exton, PA: Schiffer, 1983), 33.

36. Judi Warren Blaydon, "A Dialogue for Serious Quilters."

37. This and the following observations by Elaine Plogman are from an unpublished interview with the author, September 17, 2004.

38. Batik techniques have a long history in the Cincinnati area, where they have been taught since the early 1900s. See Boram-Hays, *Bringing Modernism Home,* 53, 222.

39. The other artists are the late Lenore Davis, Rebekka Seigel, and Jane Burch Cochran. Cochran began as a painter and later turned to quiltmaking. She and Terrie Hancock Mangat shared studio space in Cincinnati.

40. Except where otherwise noted, observations by Terrie Hancock Mangat are from an unpublished interview with the author, April 22, 2005.

41. Terrie Hancock Mangat, "A Brief History of an Artist's Studio," researched at www.terriestudio.com.

42. Terrie says, "[In the meantime] I found out what the men teachers made . . . so when he offered me another $100 raise, I looked at him and said, 'I want a $1,000 raise, or else I'm not teaching here next year,' and he gave it to me without blinking an eye, because he knew they were . . . underpaying me because I was a woman."

43. Bonnie Leman, "The Meetin' Place: Let us introduce you to Terrie Hancock Mangat of Cincinnati, Ohio," *Quilter's Newsletter Magazine,* February 1981, 26.

44. Terrie Hancock Mangat, "A Brief History of an Artist's Studio."

45. Lynn Lewis Young, "The Oklahoma City Children's Memorial Quilt Exhibition," *Art/Quilt Magazine,* no. 8 (1997): 18. For images, descriptions of artwork, and a history of the exhibition, see 16–23. Of the twenty quilts commissioned for the exhibition, five were made by Ohio and Ohio-affiliated artists: David Walker and Terrie Hancock Mangat of Cincinnati; Jane Burch Cochran of Rabbit Hash, Kentucky; Judith Vierow of Columbus; and Susan Shie and James Acord of Wooster, Ohio.

46. Michael Randles, May 24, 2005, unpublished correspondence with the author.

47. Rick Mitchell, "A Retrospective for Quilt Artist Virginia Randles," Lawrence Arts Center, Lawrence, KS, *Arts in Action* 2, no. 3 (1995): 6.

48. Virginia Randles quoted by Mitchell, "Retrospective," 6.

49. Caron L. Mosey, *Contemporary Quilts from Traditional Designs* (New York: E. P. Dutton, 1988), 41.

50. Virginia Randles, *Influences: Traditional and Contemporary Quilts,* catalog for Spencer Museum of Art, Lawrence, Kansas (Wheatridge, CO: Leman, 1983), 40.

51. Virginia Randles quoted by Mitchell, "Retrospective," 6.

52. Ibid.

53. Michael Randles, unpublished interview with the author, May 14, 2005.

54. Except where otherwise noted, observations by Sue Allen Hoyt are from an unpublished interview with the author, May 20, 2005.

55. M. J. Albacete, Sharon D'Atri, and Jane Reeves, *Ohio Quilts: A Living Tradition* (Canton, OH: Canton Art Institute, 1981), 50.

56. *Quilting II,* episode 206, hosted by Penny McMorris, Bowling Green, Ohio, WBGU-TV, 27.

57. Françoise Barnes, "Françoise Barnes: Quiltmaker and Painter," *Art/Quilt Magazine* (Winter 1996): 18.

58. Ibid., 17.

59. *Quilter's Newsletter Magazine,* January 1980, 7.

60. Except where otherwise noted, observations by Nancy Crow are from an unpublished interview with the author, August 8, 2004.

61. Nancy Crow, transcript of oral history interview conducted by Jean Robertson for the Nanette L. Laitman Documentation Project for Craft and Decorative Arts in America, Smithsonian Archives of American Art, Washington, DC, December 18, 2002. Nancy's sister Mary Crow served as poet laureate of Colorado. Her sister Martha Crow is a painter and editor.

62. Nancy Crow, *Improvisational Quilts* (Lafayette, CA: C&T Publishing, in conjunction with the Renwick Gallery of the National Museum of American Art, 1995), 3.

63. Quotations in this paragraph are from Nancy Crow, "The Meetin' Place," *Quilter's Newsletter Magazine,* July/August 1980, 22.

64. Crow, "Quilting: The Development of Art Quilts," 45.

65. Crow, "Meetin' Place," 22.

66. Crow, "Quilting: The Development of Art Quilts," 45.

67. Penny McMorris, "Reflections on Quiltmaking's Present, Part 2," *Quilter's Newsletter Magazine,* October 1994, 47.

68. Nancy Crow, *Quilts and Influences,* 91.

69. Ibid., 68.

The Big Bang and the New Universe

1. Gallery 200 in Columbus, owned by Renee Steidle, had a show in 1976, as did the Mansfield Art Center. In 1979 Kent State University exhibited art quilts in Midwest Surface Design '79; Ohio Designer Craftsmen (ODC) and Winterfair in Columbus also held art quilt exhibitions. The Cleveland Museum of Art's May Show (and affiliated Textile Art Alliance exhibits) and the Canton Art Institute's All-Ohio shows included quilts in their prestigious juried mixed-media exhibitions. In 1981 the College of Wooster held an exhibit, Ohio Quilts and Quilters, 1800–1980, which included contemporary work and lectures by Nancy Crow and Wenda von Weise; art history professor Thalia Gouma Pederson brought in Miriam Schapiro for an artist's residency, and Kent State University hosted Schapiro as well later on. Kenyon College in Gambier also held occasional exhibits of art quilts.

2. Elaine Plogman quoted by Caron L. Mosey, *Contemporary Quilts from Traditional Designs* (New York: E. P. Dutton, 1988), 62.

3. Nancy Crow, unpublished interview with the author, August 8, 2004, and Nancy Crow interview, *Ohio Pioneers of the Art Quilt* (Columbus: Ohio State University, 2003), compact disc.

4. The Ardis and Robert James Collection was donated in 1997 to the International Quilt Study Center at the University of Nebraska in Lincoln. Ohio artists in the James collection included Susan Shie, Nancy Crow, Terrie Hancock Mangat, and Elizabeth Newbill Cave. See Lynn Lewis Young, *Art/Quilt Magazine,* no. 7 (1996–97): 53. New Jersey collector James M. Walsh III began acquiring art quilts in 1990, with the help of Penny McMorris. See Gloria Hansen, "The Art of the Quilt" and "An Interview with John M. Walsh III," *Art/Quilt Magazine,* no. 7 (1996–97): 20, 21, 54.

5. Helen Cullinan quoting Penny McMorris, "Quilt Guru Curates Oberlin Exhibit," *Cleveland Plain Dealer,* June 13, 1994, 3-E.

6. Penny McMorris, "Quilting—A Reminiscence," *Lady's Circle Patchwork Quilts,* March 1986, 31.

7. Except where otherwise noted, the following observations by Penny McMorris are from an unpublished interview with the author, May 24, 2004.

8. McMorris, "Quilting—A Reminiscence," 69.

9. Ibid.

10. Bonnie Leman, "What's New—and News—In Quilting," *Quilter's Newsletter Magazine,* April 1981, 15, 23, and 34.

11. Bonnie Leman, "The Needle's Eye," *Quilter's Newsletter Magazine,* July/August 1981, 4.

12. Nancy Crow, unpublished interview with the author, August 8, 2004, and Nancy Crow interview, *Ohio Pioneers of the Art Quilt.*

13. Hilary Fletcher quoted by Louis McCormick Gibney, "Change Is What Keeps an Art Form Vital: A Visit with Hilary Morrow Fletcher," *Art/Quilt Magazine,* no. 4 (1995): 34.

14. Hilary Fletcher, unpublished interview with the author, May 4, 2004.

15. "Quilt National '79: Introduction—Part 1," Quilt National website, http://www.quiltnational.com/.

16. Michael James, "Behind the Scenes: Jurying Quilt National '79," *Quilter's Newsletter Magazine,* July/August 1979, 6.

17. The eleven Ohio artists who exhibited in the first Quilt National in 1979 are Françoise Barnes, Nancy Crow, Benita Cullinan, Lynette Janke-Weber, Terrie Hancock Mangat, Carolyn Muller, Elaine Plogman, Virginia Randles, Peggy Spaeth (a Cleveland artist and early pioneer who dropped out of the field in the mid-1980s), Mirjana Ugrinov, and Wenda von Weise. The count would rise to twelve by including Debra Millard Lunn, an artist and expert in creating hand-dyed fabrics, who moved to Ohio soon after. Lunn, a quiltmaker since 1963 who began dyeing fabric in 1976, exhibited work in the first Quilt National that was "the first and only work made of hand-dyed fabrics." Lunn and partner Michael Mrowka formed Lunn Fabrics in Lancaster, Ohio, in the early 1990s, creating high-quality one-

of-a-kind hand-dyed fabrics at a time when they were rare. (Researched at www.lunnfabrics.com.)

18. Schwindler, "Quilt National '79." The complete text of his essay is posted at the Quilt National website, http://home.frognet.net/~fletcher/quilt/qn79-intro.html.

19. Gibney, "Change."

20. Linda Fowler, unpublished interview with the author, August 4, 2004.

21. Ricky Clark, unpublished interview with the author, January 24, 2002.

22. Ricky Clark, unpublished letter to Evalena Briers, June 19, 1979.

23. Clark, a prolific author and historian in the new field of quilt historical research, "discovered quilt history" in the 1980s "and immediately knew its importance" (Clark, quoted by Jill Sell, "A Literature Found in Quilts," *Cleveland Plain Dealer*, April 21, 1998, 2-F). Clark has served on the board of FAVA and has remained active in the organization over the years, in addition to curating quilt exhibitions in the gallery space. For the exhibition Quilts and Carousels in 1983, the first she curated that included quilts, she wrote a catalog and held a symposium with speakers Jonathan Holstein, Nancy Crow, and Cuesta Benberry; she recalls that Holstein spoke about an organization in California that was doing quilt research, the American Quilt Study Group (AQSG). Clark joined AQSG and has served the organization in numerous ways over the years. Through the AQSG and other activities in Ohio, she became acquainted with Virginia Gunn of Wooster, Ohio, a quilt historian who teaches quilt history at the University of Akron.

24. Susan Jones, unpublished interview with the author, 2005. When Jones left FAVA to spend more time pursuing her artwork, Joey Rizzolo was hired as gallery director, followed by Kyle Michalak, and Gayle Pritchard became curator of Artist as Quiltmaker.

25. M. J. Albacete, Sharon D'Atri, and Jane Reeves, *Ohio Quilts: A Living Tradition* (Canton, OH: Canton Art Institute, 1981), 5. The work of the following artists was exhibited: Françoise Barnes, Marjorie Claybrook, Nancy Crow, Sue Allen Hoyt, Terrie Hancock Mangat, Carolyn Muller, Clare Murray, Joyce Parr, Elaine Plogman, Virginia Randles, Fran Soika, Peggy Spaeth, Judi Warren Blaydon, and Wenda von Weise.

26. Jane Reeves, unpublished interview with the author, July 28, 2004.

The Second Wave

1. Dean Neumann, a mathematician and Penny McMorris's husband, became interested in quilts in the early 1980s through Penny. In my interview with her, she said that he believed "that if quilters could have something so they could see what they had in their minds' eye and make changes on the screen, it would free their creativity even more." In 1991–92, when Penny was doing her third and final PBS series for WBGU-TV, *The Great American Quilt,* she presented a segment on new technology. Neumann had just finished the first version of his computer software program The Electric Quilt the night before, and presented it in the program. After the show aired, the station was inundated with phone calls, and The Electric Quilt Company was born.

2. Nancy Crow, *The Quilt: New Directions for an American Tradition,* Quilt National '83 catalog (Exton, PA: Schiffer, 1983), 7.

3. Ibid., 8.

4. Emerging Quiltmakers, Columbus Cultural Arts Center, Columbus, Ohio, February 5–29, 1984, listed in *Quilter's Newsletter Magazine,* February 1984, 13.

5. This and the following observations by Clare Murray are from an, unpublished interview with the author, July 7, 2004.

6. The members of the Dye Group are Clare Murray, Jane Reeves, Lois Carroll, Dina Schnupp, Karen Pollard, Joanne Stock, and Phyllis Bruce.

7. At the time of publication, Murray is an art professor at Malone College.

8. Robert Shaw, "Contemporary Quilts: The Walsh Collection," *Fiberarts,* January/February 2002, 39.

9. Observations by Jane Reeves are from an unpublished interview with the author, July 28, 2004.

10. Lois Carroll, an artist from Parma, Ohio, is known for her work in wearables and for her creative use of surface design approaches to create the look she desires. Friend Clare Murray says, "No one knows more techniques than Lois." Carroll was born in St. Louis, Missouri, in 1927, came

to Ohio in the 1950s, and began working in textiles after she retired from teaching.

11. Columbus artist Judith Vierow spent ten years as a weaver followed by ten years in the art quilt field creating rich narrative work. She was an early member of the Art Quilt Network, taught at QSDS, and had an impressive exhibition record. In the late 1990s she returned to painting. Vierow was born in St. Cloud, Minnesota, and came to Ohio in the 1960s to study art at Ohio State University.

12. One of Linda Fowler's early silk-screened quilts was shown in Quilt National '81. See Smith, Tanenhaus, and Holstein, *The New American Quilt*, 38.

13. Linda Fowler, "The Meetin' Place," *Quilter's Newsletter Magazine*, June 1984, 21.

14. Linda Fowler, unpublished interview with the author, August 4, 2004.

15. Nancy Crow, Quilt Network Conference, New York, New York, 1990, unpublished correspondence from Tafi Brown with the author, December 8, 2004.

16. Attendees at the "Dialogue for Serious Quilters," January 7–11, 1987, Villa Madonna, Columbus, Ohio [Ohioans are italicized]: Tafi Brown, *Nancy Crow,* Mary Jo Dalrymple, *Linda Fowler,* Janet Page Kessler, Susan Kristoferson, Esther Parkhurst, and Donna Stader. Invited but unable to attend were Virginia Jacobs, *Terrie Mangat, Susan Schroeder* (Hiram), and *Judi Warren.* Information courtesy of Tafi Brown.

17. Tafi Brown, unpublished correspondence with the author, December 8, 2004.

18. Attendees at the "Retreat for Serious Contemporary Quiltmakers," November 1987, Villa Madonna, Columbus, Ohio [Ohioans are italicized]: Tafi Brown, Vivian Choy, Anita Corum, *Nancy Crow, Sue Evenson* (Worthington), *Linda Fowler, Karen Freetage* (Canton), Rebecca Glass, Marla Hattabaugh, Virginia Jacobs (who presented a workshop), Janet Page Kessler, Dallas Koelling, Dianna Mitchell, *Clare Murray,* Jean Neblett Nagy, Jeanne Nelson, *Ruth Palmer* (Carroll), Jan Patek, *Elaine Plogman, Virginia Randles, Jane Reeves,* Julie Roseberry, *Carole Serio,* Donna Stader, *David Walker* (Cincinnati), and Barbara Watler.

19. Except where otherwise noted, observations by Deborah Melton Anderson are from an unpublished interview with the author, August 4, 2004.

20. Fowler, interview.

21. Gayle Pritchard, "Symposium Report," *Professional Quilter,* November 1990, 20.

22. Deborah Melton Anderson, "About Deborah," researched at the artist's website, www.debanderson.net.

23. Observations by Carolyn Mazloomi are from an unpublished interview with the author, July 27, 2004.

24. Except where otherwise noted, observations by David Walker are from an unpublished interview with the author, August 5, 2004.

25. David Walker, "Rejection," *Art/Quilt Magazine,* no. 2 (1995): 6.

26. David Walker, September 2001, researched on artist's website and used with permission, http://davidwalker.us/Pages/QAboutDavidWalker.html.

27. JoAnn Giordano, unpublished interview with the author, October 18, 2004.

28. Petra Soesemann, unpublished interview with the author, May 19, 2004.

29. Ibid.

30. Ann Batchelder, Libby Lehman, and Linda MacDonald, *Quilt National: Contemporary Designs in Fabric (QN '95)* (Asheville: Lark, 1995), 13.

31. Observations by Elizabeth Cave are from an unpublished interview with the author, October 1, 2004. Author's note: The artist's early work was exhibited under the name Elizabeth Newbill.

32. Except where otherwise noted, observations by Susan Shie are from an unpublished interview with the author, August 1, 2004.

33. Sandra Sider, "Folk-Art Aesthetics and American Art Quilts," *Fiberarts,* November/December 2003, 34.

34. Helen Cullinan, "No Fear of Fingerprints," *Cleveland Plain Dealer,* March 13, 1992, Section E.

35. Susan Shie, unpublished correspondence with the author, July 9, 2005.

The Millennium

1. Penny McMorris, "Quilts at the End of the '80s," *Fiberarts,* November/December 1989, 36, 39.

2. Robert Shaw, "The Art Quilt in 2003," *Fiberarts,* November/December 2003, 41.

3. Michael James, "The Digital Quilt," *Fiberarts,* November/December 2003, 26, 27, 31.

4. Gayle Pritchard, "Susan Shie and James Acord," *Professional Quilter,* Winter 1995, 22.

5. Observations by Angela White are from an unpublished interview with the author, September 16, 2004.

6. John Lefelhocz, unpublished interview with the author, July 27, 2004.

7. John Lefelhocz, quoted in Carmen Pease, "The Comeback Quilt," *Southeast Ohio Magazine,* November 21, 2003, 8, researched online at www.athensi.com.

8. Paul J. Smith, *Improvisational Quilts* (New York: C&T for the American Craft Museum, 1996), 5.

9. Nancy Crow, transcript of oral history interview conducted by Jean Robertson for the Nanette L. Laitman Documentation Project for Craft and Decorative Arts in America, Smithsonian Archives of American Art, Washington, DC, December 18, 2002, 8.

10. Jan Janeiro, "Text in Textiles," *Fiberarts,* Summer 1991, 28.

11. Sharon Bell, artist statement, July 2005.

12. Susan Krueger, artist statement, June 2005.

Conclusion

1. The exhibition, also titled The Art Quilt, was sponsored by the Art Museum Association of America and debuted at the Los Angeles Municipal Art Gallery in October 1986. Michael Kile, who lived in Ohio when he began collecting quilts in the 1970s, had moved to San Francisco and was cofounder of the *Quilt Digest,* an influential scholarly journal first published in 1983. In addition to showing quilts in beautiful color with well-written articles, the journal presented the quilts without distinguishing between antique and contemporary in terms of impact.

2. Penny McMorris, quoted in Robert Shaw, *The Art Quilt* (New York: Hugh Lauter Levin, 1997), 64.

3. Penny McMorris, "Pathways and Perspectives" symposium, Oberlin, OH; FAVA's *The Artist as Quiltmaker,* moderated by Gayle Pritchard, 2003, unpublished videotape.

4. Matthew Kangas, "A Critical Juncture: The State of the Crafts," *New Art Examiner,* September 1990, 28.

5. Brooks Barnes, "It's High Season for Blankets, But Patrons Ask: Is it Art? Competing with El Greco," *Wall Street Journal,* August 23, 2002.

6. Nancy Crow, "The Meetin' Place," *Quilter's Newsletter Magazine,* July/August 1980, 23.

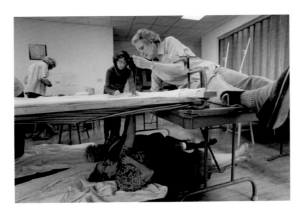

Ricky Clark and volunteers prepare a quilt for installation at FAVA's first quilt exhibition, 1983. Photo by Cindy Evans from the collection of John and Susan Edwards Harvith.

Bibliography

Exhibition, Artist, and Collections Catalogs

Albacete, M. J., Sharon D'Atri, and Jane Reeves. *Ohio Quilts: A Living Tradition.* Canton, OH: Canton Art Institute, 1981.

Angela White. Cleveland: Museum of Contemporary Art, Wendy L. Moore Emerging Artist Series, 2003.

Beds, Sweet Dreams, and Other Things. A juried surface design exhibition held in conjunction with the 1979 North Central Surface Design Association Conference, Ames, Iowa, Brunnier Gallery, Iowa State Center, 1979.

Boram-Hays, Carol. *Bringing Modernism Home: Ohio Decorative Arts 1890–1960.* Athens: Ohio University Press in conjunction with Columbus Museum of Art, 2005.

Contemporary Quilting: A Renaissance. Organized by the University of Wisconsin–Green Bay [c. 1979].

Crow, Nancy. *Nancy Crow: Improvisational Quilts.* Lafayette, CA: C&T for the Renwick Gallery of the National Museum of American Art, Smithsonian Institution, Washington, DC, 1995.

———. *Nancy Crow, Quilts and Influences.* Paducah, KY: American Quilter's Society, 1990.

Diversity! Art Quilts for the Next Century. Martinez, CA: C&T in conjunction with Studio Art Quilt Associates, 1995.

Fiber: The Artist's View. Curated by Nell Znamierowski. Greenvale, NY: Hillwood Art Gallery School of the Arts, 1983.

Fiberart International 2001. Pittsburgh, PA: Fiberarts Guild of Pittsburgh, 2001.

Gouma-Peterson, Thalia. *Miriam Schapiro: Shaping the Fragments of Art and Life.* New York: Harry N. Abrams in association with the Polk Museum of Art, 1999.

Haskell, Barbara. *The American Century: Art and Culture 1900–1950.* New York: Norton in association with the Whitney Museum of American Art, 1999.

Herman, Lloyd E. *Art That Works: Decorative Arts of the Eighties Crafted in America.* Seattle: University of Washington Press, 1990.

———. *Trashformations: Recycled Materials in Contemporary American Art and Design.* Seattle: Whatcom Museum of History and Art, 1998.

Herman, Lloyd E., and Matthew Kangas. *Tales and Traditions: Storytelling in Twentieth-Century American Craft.* St. Louis: Craft Alliance, 1993.

Holstein, Jonathan. *Abstract Design in American Quilts: A Biography of an Exhibition.* Louisville: Kentucky Quilt Project, 1991.

———. *American Pieced Quilts.* New York: Viking Press, 1973.

Influences: Traditional and Contemporary Quilts. Wheatridge, CO: Leman, 1983; catalog for Spencer Museum of Art, Lawrence, KS.

Intent '78: Fabrics. (Researched at Lark, Asheville, NC; no printing information given.)

James, Michael. *Michael James: Art and Inspirations.* Lafayette, CA: C&T, 1998.

The John M. Walsh III Collection. Lexington: University of Kentucky Art Museum, 2001.

Local Flavor. Curated by Mary Jo Bole. Cleveland: Cleveland State University, 1983.

Manhart, Marcia, and Tom Manhart, eds. *The Eloquent Object.* Seattle: University of Washington Press for the Philbrook Museum of Art, Tulsa, OK, 1987.

Miriam Schapiro: Femmages 1971–1985. St. Louis: Brentwood Gallery, 1985.

Needle Expressions '78. National Standards Council of American Embroiderers, 1978.

Needle Expressions '80. National Standards Council of American Embroiderers, 1980.

New Directions: Clay and Fiber. Greenville, NC: East Carolina University Museum of Art, 1982.

Ohio Pioneers of the Art Quilt. Columbus: Ohio State University, 2003. CD catalog with images and interviews.

Pushing the Surface 2001: Contemporary Art Quilts. Coshocton, OH: Johnson-Humrickhouse Museum, 2001.

Quilt National. *See Quilt National Exhibition Catalogs at the end of this section*

Ramsey, Bets. *A Patchwork Garden.* Chattanooga, TN: Hunter Museum of Art in conjunction with the Southern Quilt Symposium, 1981.

Ramsey, Bets, and Gail Andres Treschel. *Southern Quilts: A New View.* McLean, VA: EPM, 1991.

Robinson, Charlotte, ed. *The Artist and the Quilt.* New York: Alfred A. Knopf, 1983.

Rogers, Janet, ed. *Visions: QuiltArt.* Lafayette, CA: C&T, 1996.

Shaw, Robert, and Rachael Sadinsky. *Contemporary Art Quilts: Transformation: UCLA Alumni in Fiber.* Los Angeles: University of California, Frederich S. Wight Art Gallery, 1979.

Smith, Paul J., and Edward Lucie-Smith. *Craft Today: Poetry of the Physical.* New York: American Craft Museum: Weidenfeld and Nicolson, 1986.

Smith, Paul J., Ruth Amdur Tanenhaus, and Jonathan Holstein. *The New American Quilt.* New York: American Crafts Council, Museum of Contemporary Crafts, 1976.

Steiner, Mary Ann, and Kathryn C. Johnson, eds. *Made in America: Ten Centuries of American Art.* New York: Hudson Hills, 1995.

Timby, Deborah Bird, ed. *Visions: Quilts of a New Decade.* Lafayette, CA: C&T, 1990.

———, ed. *Visions: The Art of the Quilt.* Lafayette, CA: C&T, 1992.

Trapp, Kenneth, and Howard Risatti. *Skilled Work: American Craft in the Renwick Gallery.* Washington, DC: Smithsonian Institution Press, 1998.

Ward, Evelyn Svec, June M. Bonner, and Donna van Dijk. *Fiberworks.* Cleveland: Cleveland Museum of Art, 1977.

Quilt National Exhibition Catalogs:

The New American Quilt. Asheville, NC: Fiberarts/Lark Books in conjunction with Quilt National, 1981.

The Quilt: New Directions for an American Tradition: Quilt National. Exton, PA: Schiffer, 1983.

Quilts: The State of an Art: Quilt National. West Chester, PA: Schiffer, 1985.

Fiber Expressions: The Contemporary Quilt: Quilt National. West Chester, PA: Schiffer, 1987.

New Quilts: Interpretations and Innovations: Quilt National. West Chester, PA: Schiffer, 1989.

The New Quilt 1: Dairy Barn Quilt National. Newtown, CT: Taunton, 1991.

The New Quilt 2: Dairy Barn: Quilt National. Newtown, CT: Taunton, 1993.

Quilt National: Contemporary Designs in Fabric. Asheville, NC: Lark Books, 1995.

Contemporary Quilts: Quilt National 1997. Asheville, NC: Lark Books, 1997.

The Best in Contemporary Quilts: Quilt National 1999. Asheville, NC: Lark Books, 1999.

The Best of Contemporary Quilts: Quilt National 2001. New York: Lark Books, 2001.

Quilt National 2003: The Best of Contemporary Quilts. New York: Lark Books, 2003.

Art and Craft

Allrich, Louise Barco. "Where Do We Go from Here?" *Fiberarts,* Summer 1998, 30–35.

Anderson, Deborah. "Liturgical Quilting." *American Quilter,* Summer 1991, 17–20.

"The Artist as Quiltmaker: Pathways and Perspectives Symposium," Firelands Association for the Visual Arts, Oberlin, OH, 2002, curated and moderated by Gayle Pritchard. Unpublished VHS format.

Art/Quilt Magazine, 1994–2000.

Avery, Virginia. *The Big Book of Appliqué.* New York: Charles Scribner, 1978.

———. *Quilts to Wear.* New York: Charles Scribner, 1982.

Barnes, Françoise. "Françoise Barnes: Quiltmaker and Painter." *Art/Quilt Magazine* (Winter 1996): 17–19.

Barrie, Dennis. *Artists in Residence: Wenda von Weise.* Cleveland: New Organization for the Visual Arts, February 14, 1984. VHS format.

Benberry, Cuesta. "The Story-Tellers: African-American Quilts Come to the Fore." *Quilter's Newsletter Magazine,* November 1990, 46, 47.

———. "The 20th Century's First Quilt Revival, Part I: The Interim Period." *Quilter's Newsletter Magazine,* July/August 1979, 20–22.

———. "The 20th Century's First Quilt Revival, Part II: The First Quilt Revival." *Quilter's Newsletter Magazine,* September 1979, 25, 26, 29.

———. "The 20th Century's First Quilt Revival, Part III: The World War I Era." *Quilter's Newsletter Magazine,* October 1979, 10, 11, 37.

Bender, Marilyn. "Craft Comeback." *New York Times,* March 28, 1971, F2.

Bole-Becker, Luanne, and Bob Bole-Becker. *Unraveling the Stories: Quilts as a Reflection of Our Lives.* Lakewood, OH: BB Sound and Light, 1998. VHS format.

Brackman, Barbara. "Memories: Looking Back at Five Years of Quilting Events." *Quilter's Newsletter Magazine,* September 1989, 32–34, 51.

Broude, Norma, and Mary D. Garrard, eds. *Feminism and Art History: Questioning the Litany,* New York: Harper and Row, 1982.

———, eds. *The Power of Feminist Art: The American Movement of the 1970s, History and Impact.* New York: Harry N. Abrams, 1994.

Broun, Elizabeth, Kenneth R. Trapp, and Howard Risatti. *Skilled Work: American Craft in the Renwick Gallery.* Washington, DC: Smithsonian Institution Press, 1998.

Brown, Tafi. "The Studio Art Quilt: Perspectives on a Movement." *Surface Design Journal,* Spring 1992, 16.

Chambers, Karen. "Wearable Art." *AmericanStyle,* Spring 1998, 48, 51–53.

Chase, Patti, with Mimi Dolbier. *The Contemporary Quilt: New American Quilts and Fabric Art.* New York: E. P. Dutton, 1978.

Crow, Nancy. "Quilting: The Development of Art Quilts." *Fiberarts,* January/February 1990, 44–47.

Cullinan, Helen. "No Fear of Fingerprints." *Cleveland Plain Dealer,* March 13, 1993, E-1.

Dale, Julie Schafler. "Wearables: Developments and Trends." *Fiberarts,* January/February 1990, 42, 43.

Davis, Douglas. "Art as Act." *Art in America,* March/April 1970, 31.

DeLong, Kathryn, ed. "2003 Awards of Achievement: Visual Arts: Angela White." *Northern Ohio Live,* October 2003, A35.

Farkas, Maxine. "Quilt National '01." *Fiberarts,* November/December 2001, 54, 55.

Fiberarts Design Book. Asheville, NC: Fiberarts, 1980.

Fiberarts Design Book II. Edited by Jeane Hutchins. Asheville, NC: Lark Books, 1983.

Fiberarts Design Book III. Edited by Kate Mathews. Asheville, NC: Lark Books, 1987.

Fiberworks: Symposium on Contemporary Textile Art, May 12–14, 1978, Merritt College, Oakland, Calif. Berkeley, CA: Fiberworks, 1978.

Fletcher, Hilary Morrow. "Letters: Quilt National '01." *Fiberarts,* January/February 2002, 7.

Friedland, Shirley, and Leslie Piña. *Wearable Art, 1900–2000.* Atglen, PA: Schiffer 1999.

Freudenheim, Betty. "Defining Contemporary Quilts." *Fiberarts,* Summer 1991, 48, 50.

Glueck, Grace. "They're Shoofly and Crazy, Man." *New York Times,* June 27, 1971, D24.

Gutcheon, Beth. "Art for Use." *American Craft,* April/May 1980, 8–11.

———. *The Perfect Patchwork Primer.* New York: David McKay, 1973.

———. "Quilt National '79." *Fiberarts,* September/October 1979, 80–82.

Halpern, Nancy. "The State—and Future—of the Art Quilt." *Lady's Circle Patchwork Quilts,* #22, 1981, 59–60.

Harriss, Joseph. "The Newest Quilt Fad Seems to Be Going Like Crazy." *Smithsonian,* May 1987, 114–116, 118, 120–123.

Holstein, Jonathan. *The Pieced Quilt: An American Design Tradition.* New York: Galahad Books, 1973.

James, Michael. "The Digital Quilt." *Fiberarts,* November/December 2003, 26–31.

———. "Getting Our Bearings: Quilt Art at Century's End." *American Quilter,* Fall 1992, 52–54, 74.

———. *The Quiltmaker's Handbook: A Guide to Design and Construction.* Englewood Cliffs, NJ: Prentice Hall, 1978.

———. *The Second Quiltmaker's Handbook: Creative Approaches to Contemporary Quilt Design.* Englewood Cliffs, NJ: Prentice Hall, 1981.

Janeiro, Jan. "Katherine Westphal and the Creative Process." *Fiberarts,* November/December, 1980, 35–37.

Kangas, Matthew. "A Critical Juncture: The State of the Crafts." *New Art Examiner,* September 1990, 28.

Kiracofe, Roderick. *The American Quilt: A History of Cloth and Comfort 1750–1950.* New York: Clarkson Potter, 1993.

Kramer, Hilton. "Art: Quilts Find a Place at the Whitney." *New York Times,* July 3, 1971, 22.

Lady's Circle Patchwork Quilts, No. 15: Art Quilts Collector's Edition. New York: Lopez 1990.

Laury, Jean Ray. *Imagery on Fabric.* 2nd ed. Lafayette, CA: C&T, 1997.

———. *Quilted Clothing.* Birmingham, AL: Oxmoor House, 1982.

———. *Quilts and Coverlets: A Contemporary Approach.* New York: Van Nostrand Reinhold, 1970.

Lawson, Carol. "Quilts: New Esthetic, New Craftsmen, New Collectors." *New York Times,* January 28, 1988, C1.

Levin, Elaine. "Judy Chicago's Dinner Party." *Craft Horizons,* April 1979, 53–55.

Lippard, Lucy R. "Sexual politics, art style." *Art in America,* September/October 1971, 19, 20.

Lovelace, Carey. "Feminism at 40: Recent Overlapping Exhibitions in New York City and East Hampton Explored First-Generation Feminist Art and Its Legacy—Art & Politics I—Critical Essay." *Art in America,* May 2003, accessed at www.findarticles.com.

Lucie-Smith, Edward. *Movements in Art since 1945.* New York: Thames and Hudson, 2001.

———. *The Story of Craft: The Craftsman's Role in Society.* Ithaca, NY: Cornell University Press/Phaidon Books, 1981.

Lynes, Russell. "Revival of the Fittest." *Art in America,* March/April 1970, 27.

Mainardi, Patricia. *Quilts: The Great American Art.* San Pedro, CA: Miles and Weir, 1978.

Malarcher, Patricia. "In Search of 'Quiltness.'" *Surface Design Journal,* Spring 1992, 8–11.

Martin, Lois. "The Making of Quilts, The Maker of Quilts." *American Craft,* June/July 1995, 32.

Mattera, Joanne. "Judy Chicago's Dinner Party." *Fiberarts,* May/June 1980, 16, 84.

———, ed. *The Quiltmaker's Art: Contemporary Quilts and Their Makers.* Asheville, NC: Lark Books, 1982.

Mazloomi, Carolyn. *Spirits of the Cloth: Contemporary African American Quilts.* New York: Clarkson N. Potter, 1998.

McCann, Kathleen. "Trends in Fiber Art." *Fiberarts,* March/April 1990, 38–40.

McMorris, Penny. "A New Generation of Quilts." *Creative Ideas for Living,* January 1987, 19, 20.

———. "Quilting—A Reminiscence." *Lady's Circle Patchwork Quilts,* March 1986, 30, 31, 68, 69.

———. *Quilting with Penny McMorris.* Bowling Green, OH: WBGU-TV and Bowling Green State University, 1981.

———. *Quilting II with Penny McMorris.* Bowling Green, OH: WBGU-TV and Bowling Green State University, 1982.

———. "Quilts at the End of the '80s." *Fiberarts,* November/December 1989, 36–39.

———. "Reflections on Quiltmaking's Future." *Quilter's Newsletter Magazine,* November 1994, 48–51.

———. "Reflections on Quiltmaking's Past." *Quilter's Newsletter Magazine,* September 1994, 28–31.

———. "Reflections on Quiltmaking's Present." *Quilter's Newsletter Magazine,* October 1994, 44–47.

McMorris, Penny, and Michael Kile. *The Art Quilt.* San Francisco: Quilt Digest Press, 1986; 2nd ed., Chicago: Quilt Digest, 1996.

Mosey, Caron L. *Contemporary Quilts from Traditional Designs.* New York: E. P. Dutton, 1988.

O'Dowd, Karen. "The Eye of the Beholder." *Lady's Circle Art Quilts,* #15, 1990, 72–74.

Pattison, Darcy S. "Quilt National, A Decade of Growth for the Art Quilt." *Quilting Today,* August/September 1989, 54–59.

Pease, Carmen. "The Comeback Quilt." *Southeast Ohio Magazine,* November 21, 2003, accessed at www.athensi.com.

Penders, Mary Coyne. "Journeys Through the World of Quilts." *Quilter's Newsletter Magazine,* November/December 1989, 20, 68.

Pritchard, Gayle. "The Future of Quilts as Art." *American Quilter,* Spring 1992, 8–9.

———. "Susan Shie and James Acord." *Professional Quilter,* Winter 1995, 13, 22.

———. "Symposium Report." *Professional Quilter,* November 1990, 20.

Professional Quilter, 1985–1994.

Pulleyn, Rob. "Goodbye from Rob Pulleyn." *Fiberarts,* March/April 2004, accessed at www.fiberartsmagazine.com.

Quilt Digest, 1983–86.

Robinson, Sharon. *Contemporary Quilting.* Worcester, MA: Davis, 1982.

Schroeder, Rosalie. "Sister Linda Fowler." *Professional Quilter,* August 1989, 7.

Seckler, Dorothy Gees. "Artists in America: Victim of the Culture Boom?" *Art in America,* November/December 1963, 28–39.

Seelig, Warren. "Technology and the Hand." *Surface Design Journal,* Fall 2003, 6–9.

Shaw, Robert. *The Art Quilt.* New York: Hugh Lauter Levin, 1997.

Shaw, Robert, interviewed by Sunita Patterson. "The Art Quilt in 2003." *Fiberarts,* November/December 2003, 37.

———. "Contemporary Quilts: The Walsh Collection." *Fiberarts,* January/February 2002, 35–39.

Sider, Sandra. "Folk-Art Aesthetics and American Art Quilts." *Fiberarts,* November/December 2003, 32–36.

Spears, Darcey M. "Is Quilting Art?" *Professional Quilter,* August 1986, 6–10.

Tabah, May Natalie. "If God had wanted a woman to be a Genius He'd have made her a man." *Craft Horizons,* June 1978, 25, 68, 69.

Talley, Charles. "Quilt Talk: A Conversation with Shelly Zegart." *Surface Design Journal,* Summer 1993, 35, 37.

Tuchman, Maurice. "Art and Technology." *Art in America,* March/April 1970, 78.

Warren, Judi. *Fabric Postcards: Landmarks and Landscapes, Monuments and Meadows.* Paducah, KY: American Quilter's Society, 1994.

Young, Lynn Lewis. "Linda Fowler: New Life Series." *Art/Quilt Magazine,* no. 1 (1994): 31, 35.

History, General

Benberry, Cuesta. "White Perspectives of Blacks in Quilts and Related Media." *Uncoverings: The Research Papers of the American Quilt Study Group* 4 (1983): 59–74.

Bird, Caroline. *The Invisible Scar: The Great Depression.* New York: David McKay, 1966.

Carow, Barbara. "Art Quilt Makers and Their Critique Groups." *Uncoverings: The Research Papers of the American Quilt Study Group* 18 (1997): 41–65.

Clark, Ricky, George W. Knepper, and Ellice Ronsheim. *Quilts in Community.* Nashville, TN: Rutledge Hill, 1991.

Cullinan, Helen. "Solver of Quilt Puzzles." *Cleveland Plain Dealer,* October 30, 1994, 2-J.

Ducey, Carolyn, and Mary Ellen Ducey. "Quilt Symposium '77: 'Fine Art–Folk Art' at Lincoln, Nebraska." *Uncoverings: The Research Papers of the American Quilt Study Group* 24 (2003): 75–97.

Farber, David, ed. *The Sixties: From Memory to History.* Chapel Hill: University of North Carolina Press, 1994.

Gittler, Adele. "Love-Letter in Thread." *Elyria (Ohio) Chronicle-Telegram,* May 19, 1974, C-1.

Gunn, Virginia, Ricky Clark, and Stephanie N. Tan. *Treasures from Trunks: Early Quilts from Wayne and Holmes Counties.* College of Wooster Art Museum catalog, Wooster, OH: Collier, 1987.

Gutcheon, Jeffrey. "Finished Fabrics." *Quilter's Newsletter Magazine,* January 1982, 14, 18.

———. "Notes Toward a History of Modern Quilting." *Quilter's Newsletter Magazine,* January/February 1991, 14, 62.

Hall-Patton, Colleen R. "Innovation among Southern California Quilters: An Anthropological Perspective." *Uncoverings: The Research Papers of the American Quilt Study Group* 8 (1987): 73–86.

Harter, Kevin. "Quilters Refine Their Craft to an Art." *Cleveland Plain Dealer,* November 19, 1992, 4-B.

Hilty, Lucille. "A Passion for Quiltmaking." *Uncoverings: The Research Papers of the American Quilt Study Group* 1 (1980): 13–17.

Janeiro, Jan. "Text in Textiles." *Fiberarts,* Summer 1991, 28–31.

Jenkins, Susan, and Linda Seward. *The American Quilt Story: The How-To and Heritage of a Craft Tradition.* Emmaus, PA: Rodale, 1991.

Jessen, Carol. "Stitches That Do More Than Bind." *Fiberarts,* November/December 1991, 43–47.

Knepper, George W. *Ohio and Its People.* 2nd ed. Kent, OH: Kent State University Press, 1997.

Langellier, Kristin M. "Contemporary Quiltmaking in Maine: Re-fashioning Femininity." *Uncoverings: The Research Papers of the American Quilt Study Group* 11 (1990): 29–55.

Leman, Bonnie. "The Meetin' Place: Nancy Crow, Baltimore, Ohio." *Quilter's Newsletter Magazine,* July/August 1980, 22, 23.

Many, Paul. "Athens Tapestry Works." *Fiberarts,* July/August 1978, 51–52.

McMillan, Patricia. "The Meetin' Place: Sr. Linda Fowler of Columbus, Ohio." *Quilter's Newsletter Magazine,* June 1984, 21, 43.

Neptune, Jeanne. "Where You'll Find Me: Quiltmaking on the Internet." *Art/Quilt Magazine,* no. 7 (1996): 32–33.

Orlofsky, Patsy, and Myron Orlofsky. *Quilts in America.* New York: Abbeville, 1992.

Przybysz, Jane. "The Body En(w)raptured: Contemporary Quilted Garments." *Uncoverings: The Research Papers of the American Quilt Study Group* 10 (1989): 102–22.

———. "Competing Cultural Values at The Great American Quilt Festival." *Uncoverings: The Research Papers of the American Quilt Study Group* 8 (1987): 107–27.

Rake, Valerie S. "A Thread of Continuity: Quiltmaking in Wayne County, Ohio Mennonite Churches, 1890s–1990s." *Uncoverings: The Research Papers of the American Quilt Study Group* 20 (1999): 31–62.

Schulman, Bruce J. *The Seventies.* Cambridge, MA: Da Capo, 2002.

Sell, Jill. "A Literature Found in Quilts." *Cleveland Plain Dealer,* April 21, 1998, 2-F.

Spears, Jeannie M. "Teacher of the Year, 1991." *Professional Quilter,* May 1991, 3–5.

Stern, Jane, and Michael Stern. *Sixties People.* New York: Alfred A. Knopf, 1990.

Waldvogel, Merikay. *Soft Covers for Hard Times: Quiltmaking and the Great Depression.* Nashville, TN: Rutledge Hill, 1990.

Woodard, Thos. K., and Blanche Greenstein. *Twentieth Century Quilt: 1900–1950.* New York: E. P. Dutton, 1988.

Zinn, Howard. *The Twentieth Century: A People's History.* New York: Harper and Row, 1984.

Zlotnik, Cynthia. "The Meetin' Place: Susan Shie of Wooster, Ohio." *Quilter's Newsletter Magazine,* July/August 1990, 40, 41.

Studio of Nancy Crow, 2004. The raw materials await the artist's hand. Photo by Haley Pritchard.

Index